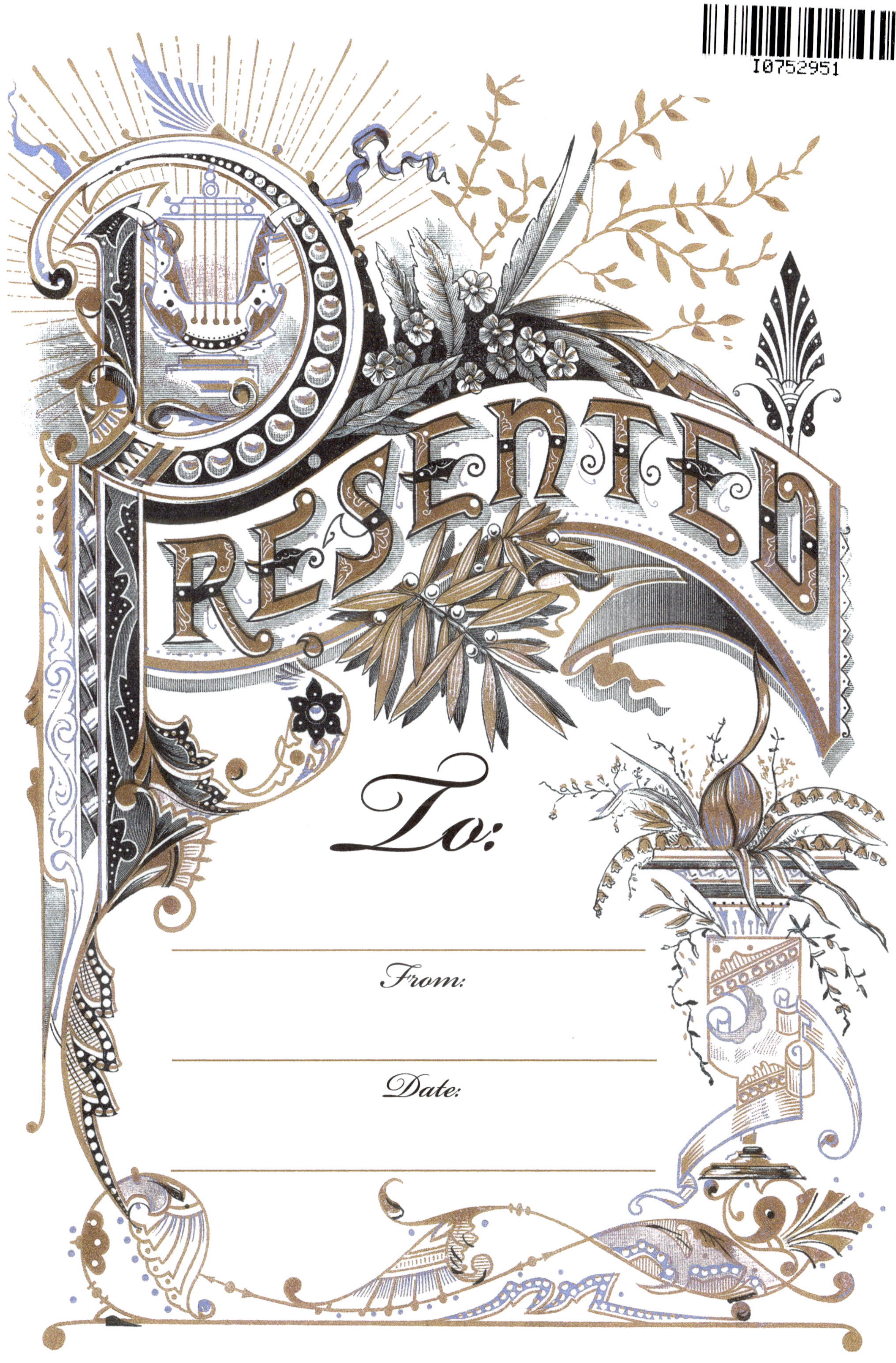
Presented
To:
From:
Date:

Old Testament
BIBLE STORY ILLUSTRATIONS

An Adult Coloring Book
of Antique Engravings

Linda Wright

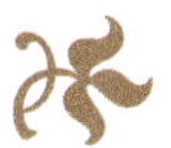

Classic Bookwrights
Santa Barbara, California

Also by Classic Bookwrights:

New Testament Bible Story Illustrations: An Adult Coloring Book of Antique Engravings by Linda Wright
Bible Stores for Children: Classic Bible Stories Every Child Should Know by Jesse Lyman Hurlbut
The Mary Frances Sewing Book 100th Anniversary Edition by Jane Eayre Fryer

Illustrations and Bible Stories are from
Charming Bible Stories by Henry Davenport Northrup, D.D.
published by J.H.Moore, 1894.

This special collection of antique illustrations has been carefully restored with
state-of-the-art equipment and techniques for 21st century colorists.
Scanned, restored, edited and arranged by Linda Wright.

Classic Bookwrights
P.O. Box 90135
Santa Barbara, California 93190
info@ClassicBookwrights.com

Version: 2.0

ISBN: 978-1-937564-08-7

Introduction

This book is a collection of beloved Bible stories as much as it is a coloring book. From Adam and Eve and Noah's Ark to Moses receiving the Ten Commandments and beyond, you can share in these recorded experiences and bring them to life with color. To enhance your enjoyment of coloring a page, each exquisite illustration is back-printed with an excerpt from the Bible story it depicts. Coloring Bible stories provides an opportunity for reflection and quiet inspiration along with the creativity of coloring. Each page is printed on 70 lb. premium-weight paper that is acid free.

The drawings in this book have been shaded using the artistic techniques of hatching and cross-hatching. Simply color over these areas and allow the patterns below to show through. For further depth, additional shading can be applied on top. You may also find parts of certain drawings to be too detailed to color in every little area, so in that case, you may also choose to color over the top. For adding color, markers and colored pencils work well. For intricate details, try fine tip gel pens.

Test your media on a piece of scrap paper before starting on the artwork to be sure you are happy with the look. When coloring with pencils, start with a light touch. You can always go back and deepen the shade with more pressure and more layers but it's not so easy to lighten.

You will want a sharp point to color small areas with colored pencils so keep a pencil sharpener nearby. Any kind of pencil sharpener can be used. A small hand-held manual sharpener will give you the best control to smoothly sharpen your colored pencils to just the right point.

To remove a page for coloring, use a utility knife. Otherwise, if you are coloring with the pages in the book, place a protective layer of paper or cardstock behind your work to catch any color that bleeds through. To keep your borders free of overspill, low-tack artist tape can be used to mask off the edges.

Thank you so much for buying my book. Restoring these beautiful illustrations was truly a labor of love and I hope you enjoy coloring them. If you enjoy the book, please consider leaving a review at your online place of purchase to help others. ***Old Testament Bible Story Illustrations***, and its companion book, ***New Testament Bible Story Illustrations***, are inspirational coloring books. May you find hours of tranquility and refreshment as you create your own masterpieces of beauty and devotion.

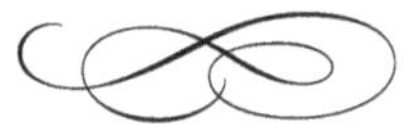

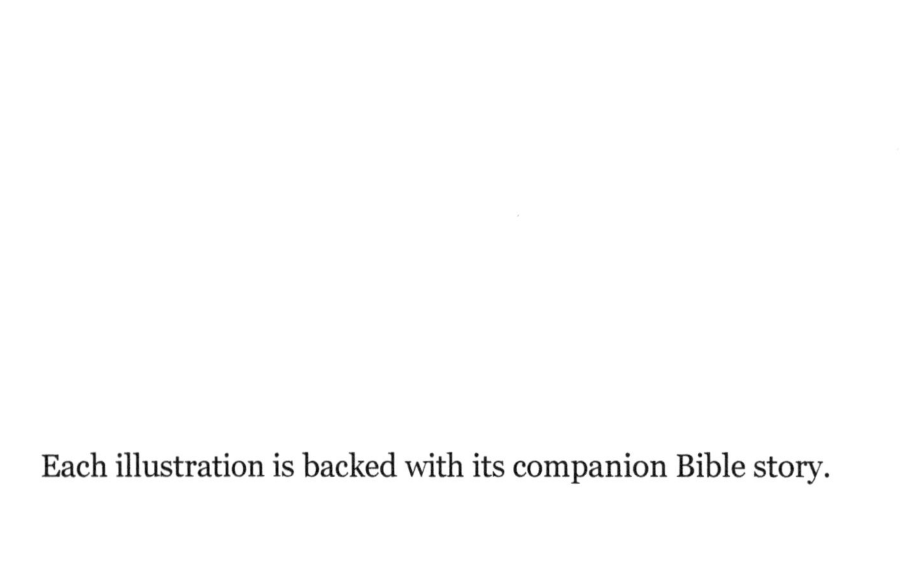

Each illustration is backed with its companion Bible story.

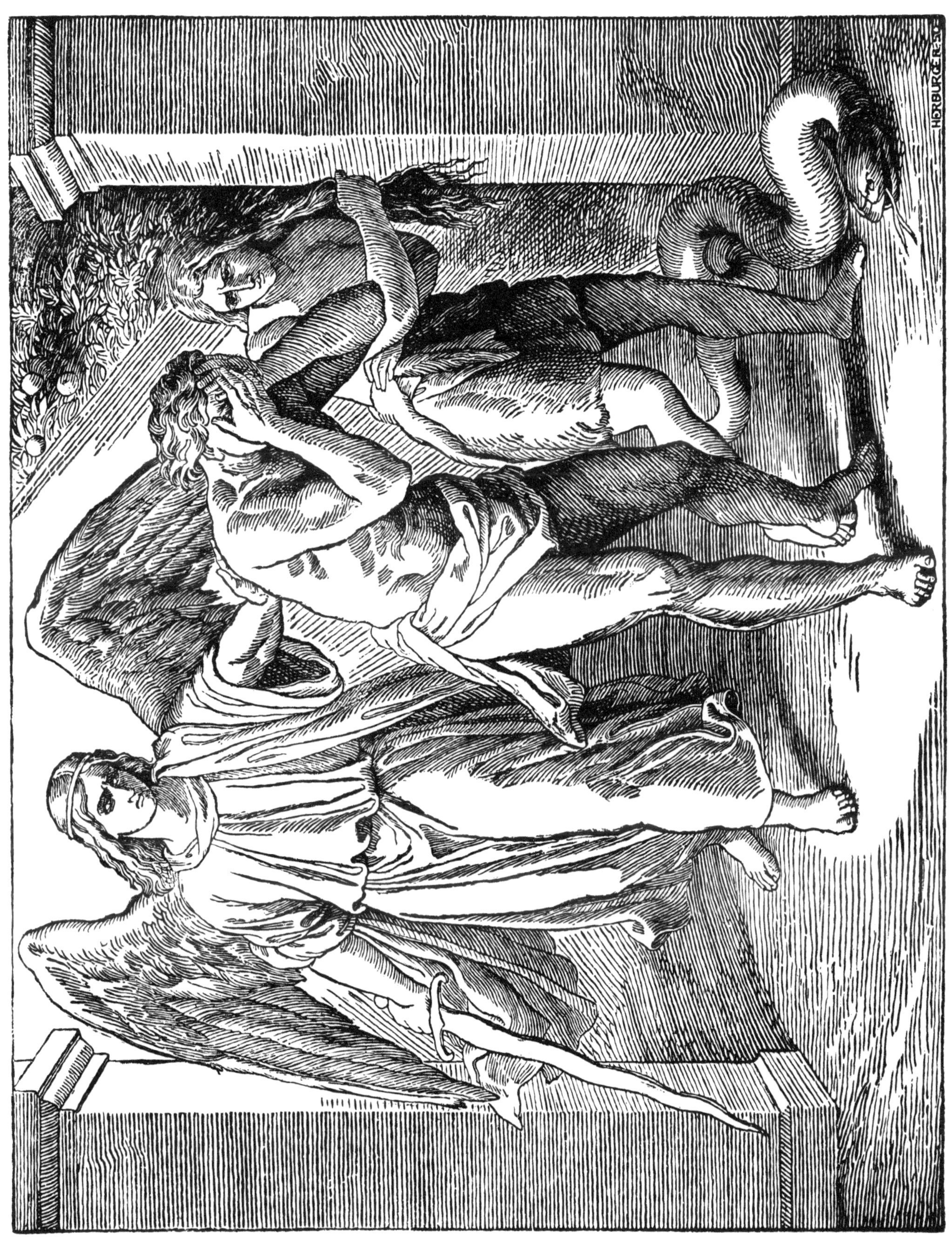

Adam and Eve Driven Out of the Garden of Eden

And God said unto Adam, Because thou hast hearkened unto the voice of thy wife, and hast eaten of the tree of the knowledge of good and evil, cursed is the ground for thy sake; in sorrow shalt thou eat of it all the days of thy life, till thou return unto the ground; for out of it wast thou taken: for dust thou art, and unto dust shalt thou return. Adam called his wife's name Eve; because she was the mother of all the living. And the Lord God said, Behold, the man is become as one of us, to know good and evil: and now the Lord God shall send him forth from the garden of Eden to till the ground from whence he was taken.

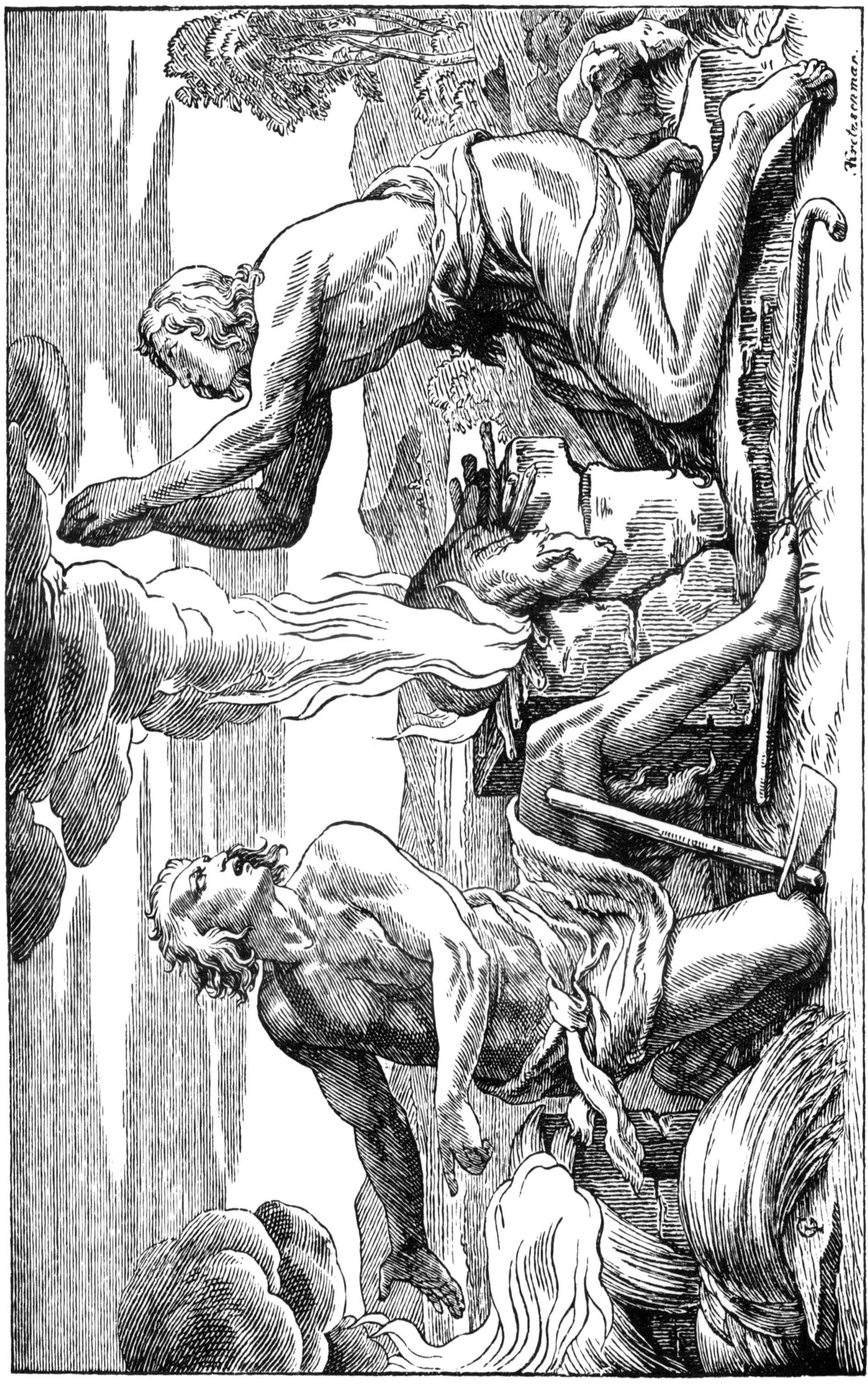

Cain and Abel Making an Offering to the Lord

After they left the Garden of Eden, Adam and Eve had two sons: the eldest was called Cain, and was a tiller of the ground; but the younger was called Abel, and was a keeper of sheep. Now both brothers made offerings to the Lord: Cain offered of the fruits of the field and Abel of the firstlings of his flock. And the Lord had respect unto Abel and to his offering. But unto Cain and his offering, he had not respect. At this Cain became very wroth, and his countenance fell. And the Lord said, Why art thou wroth, and why is thy countenance fallen? If thou doest well shalt thou not also receive a reward? But if thou doest not well, sin lieth at the door.

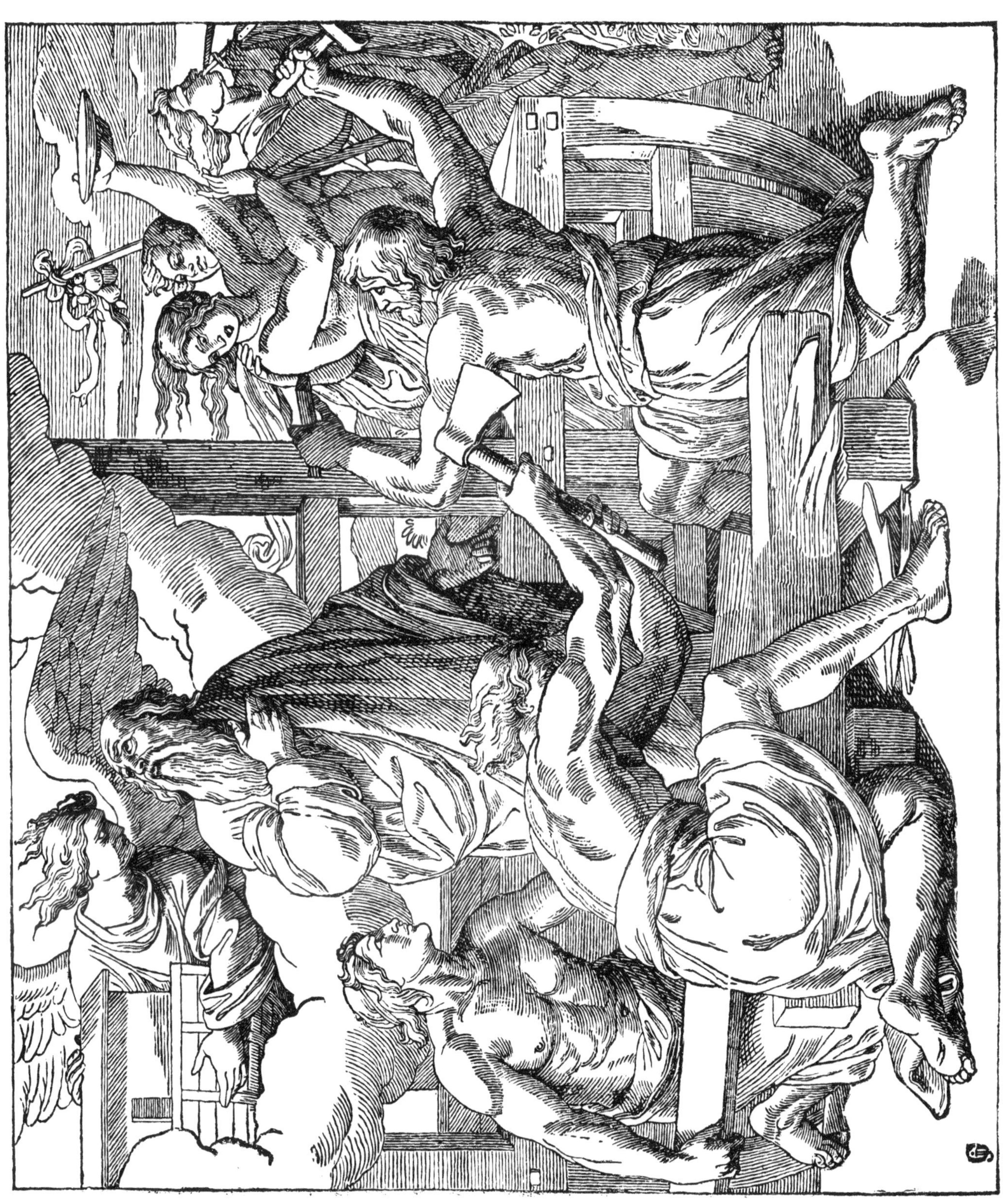

Noah Building the Ark

A great many years passed, and there was a multitude of people in the world. They had become very wicked, and were growing more so. And God looked upon the earth, and he saw that the wickedness of man was very great, and that the thoughts of his heart were evil. And the Lord said, I will destroy man whom I have created from the face of the earth; both man, and beast, and the creeping thing, and the fowls of the air; for I am sorry that I made them.

There was only one man amongst them all at this time who pleased God, and his name was Noah. He found favor in the eyes of the Lord; for he was a good man. He walked with God, and he had brought up his children wisely and well.

So God spoke to Noah and told him what he was going to do. He said, Behold, I will bring a flood of waters upon the earth, to destroy by drowning everything that breathes; and everything that is on the earth shall die. But I will take care of you, and your wife, and your sons, and your sons' wives.

Then he told Noah to make a very large boat called an "ark" which should float upon the water. And into this ark, Noah and his family were to go, with two of every sort of living creature, that they might be kept alive. An abundance of food was to be put into the ark for them all. Noah began at once to make the ark. And all the time the ark was being made, for it took a great many years, Noah preached to the people, and warned them. He told them that God was going to drown the world for their wickedness; but they did not believe him. They went on eating and drinking and pleasing themselves, and doing everything just as usual.

And so year after year passed away. Noah still worked hard at the ark, which was to save him and his family, and he still went on preaching and warning his neighbors, until the great ark was finished.

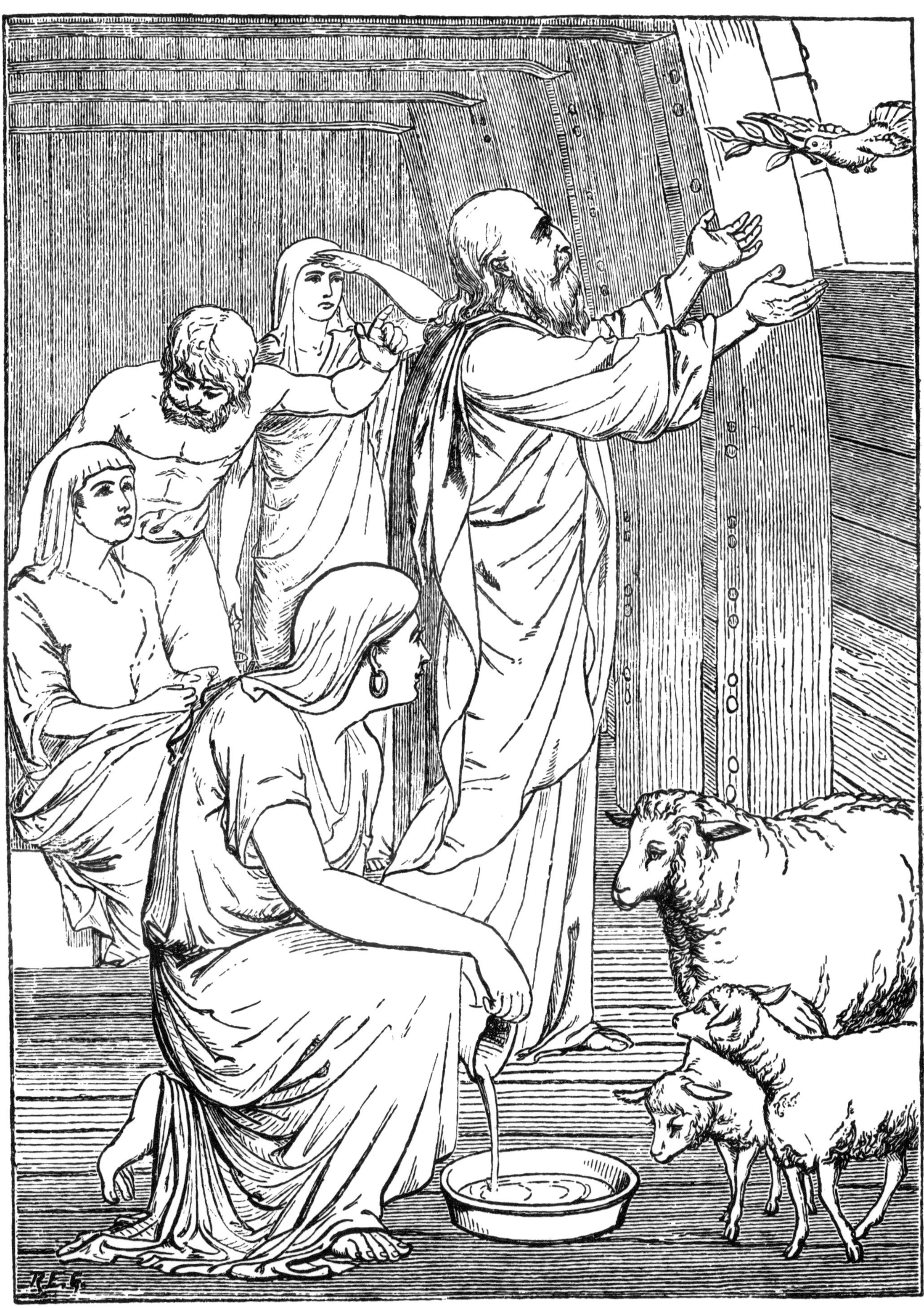

Return of the Dove to the Ark

After forty days of rain, God made the rain to cease, and he caused a wind to pass over the earth, to help to dry up the waters. Noah wanted very much to know if the earth was getting dry again; for though there was a window in the ark, it was placed so that he could not see anything out of it except the sky. He could open it, however; and so one day he took a raven and let it out through the window. But the raven did not come back; it flew backward and forward over the water, and rested on the top of the ark, but it would not go into it again. Then Noah sent out a dove, which is a very gentle bird — very different to the wild and fierce raven. But the dove found no tree upon which she could perch, and no place where she could rest, so she flew back to the ark. And Noah was watching for her, and when he saw her come back, he put out his hand and took her gently in through the window. After this Noah waited one week, and then he sent out the dove again. The gentle bird did not come back quite so soon this time. She remained away till the evening; and when she returned to the ark, she had an olive leaf in her beak that she had plucked off a tree. Noah was pleased to see it, for he knew by this that the flood of waters had almost gone.

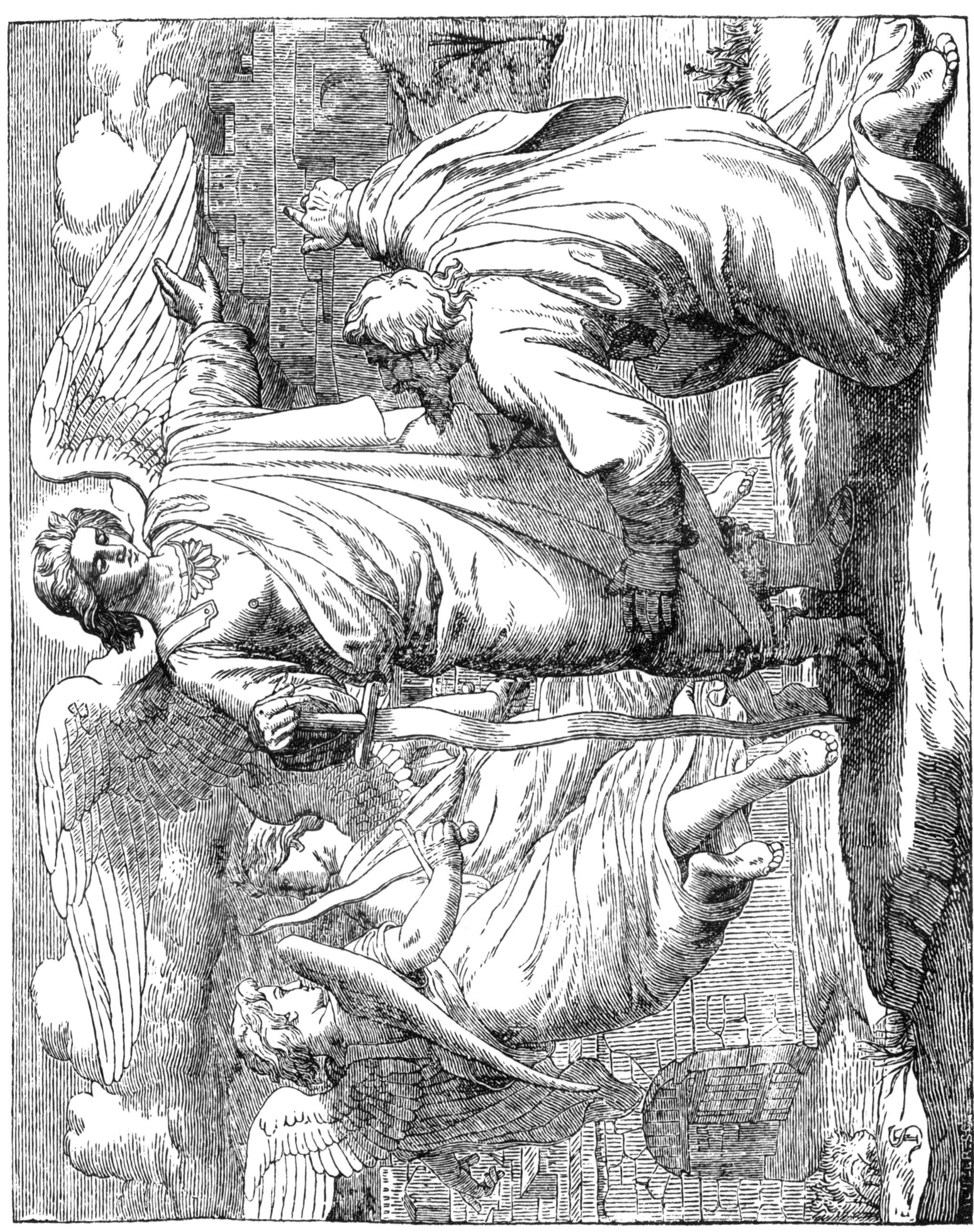

The Destruction of Sodom Foretold to Abraham

The Lord said to Abraham, because the report of the cities of Sodom and Gomorrah is very evil, and their sin very grievous, I have come to see whether they have altogether sinned according to the report.

Abraham stood before the Lord. He thought of Lot, his brother's son, and of his household, and said to the Lord, Will thou also destroy the righteous with the wicked? What if there are fifty righteous within the city; will thou not spare the place for the sake of the fifty righteous? That be far from thee to slay the righteous with the wicked. Shall not the Judge of all the earth do right? The Lord said, If I find in Sodom fifty righteous, I will spare all the place for their sake.

Abraham spake again, I have taken upon myself to speak to the Lord, though I be but dust and ashes. What if there are forty and five righteous people: wilt thou destroy all the city for the lack of five?

The Lord said, If I find forty and five, I will not destroy it.

Abraham said again, What if forty are found there?

And the Lord answered, I will not do it if there be forty there.

Then Abraham said, Let not the Lord be angry, and I will speak. What if thirty are found there?

The Lord said, I will not do it if I find thirty there.

Abraham spake again, What if twenty are found there?

The Lord answered, I will spare it for twenty's sake.

Yet once again did Abraham speak. Let not the Lord be angry, and I will speak but this once only. What if ten are found there? And the Lord said, I will spare it for ten's sake. Then Abraham was satisfied; he left off praying for Sodom, and returned to his home.

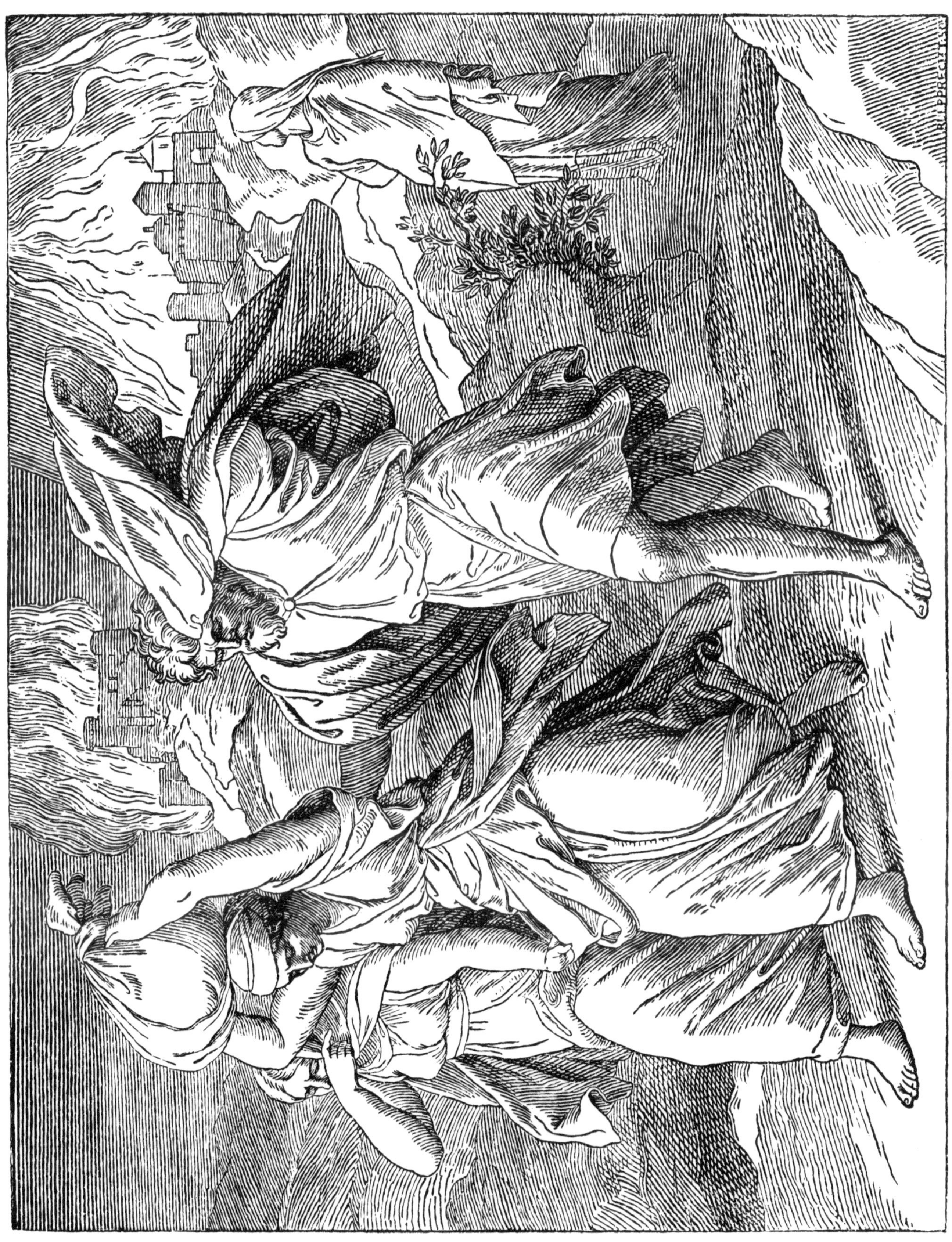

Lot and His Family Fleeing from Sodom

The angels that God had sent to Sodom came in the evening. They met Lot in the gate of the city. Lot thought they were two men who were on a journey. He therefore asked them to stay in his house that night, and prepared supper for them, and treated them kindly. The angels found that all the other men of the city cared for nothing but wickedness, and they said to Lot, Have you sons or daughters in the city besides those in this house? If you have, bring them out of the place, for the wickedness of it is become great before the Lord and he has sent us to destroy it. All the good people in the city could save their lives by leaving at once.

Lot went out and said to the men who had married his daughters, Up! get you out of this place, for the Lord will destroy it. But they would not believe him. When the morning dawned, the angels hastened Lot and said, Arise, take your wife and your two daughters that are here, and get away, lest you be destroyed in the punishment of the city. Strange to say, he still delayed; but the angels caught them by the hand, and brought them out of the city, and said, Escape for your life; do not look behind you nor stop anywhere in the plain; escape to the mountain, lest you be consumed.

Lot feared to go to the mountain, and he said, There is a little city in this plain; let me stay there. It is but a little one; will not God spare it? And the angel said, I will not overthrow the city for which you have spoken. Hasten! escape to it; for I cannot do anything till you are come into it. The name of the little city was Zoar. As soon as Lot came into it, the Lord rained upon Sodom and Gomorrah brimstone and fire out of heaven, and overthrew those cities, and all the inhabitants of the plain, and everything that grew upon the ground. But Lot's wife turned and looked back upon the burning cities, and she became a pillar of salt.

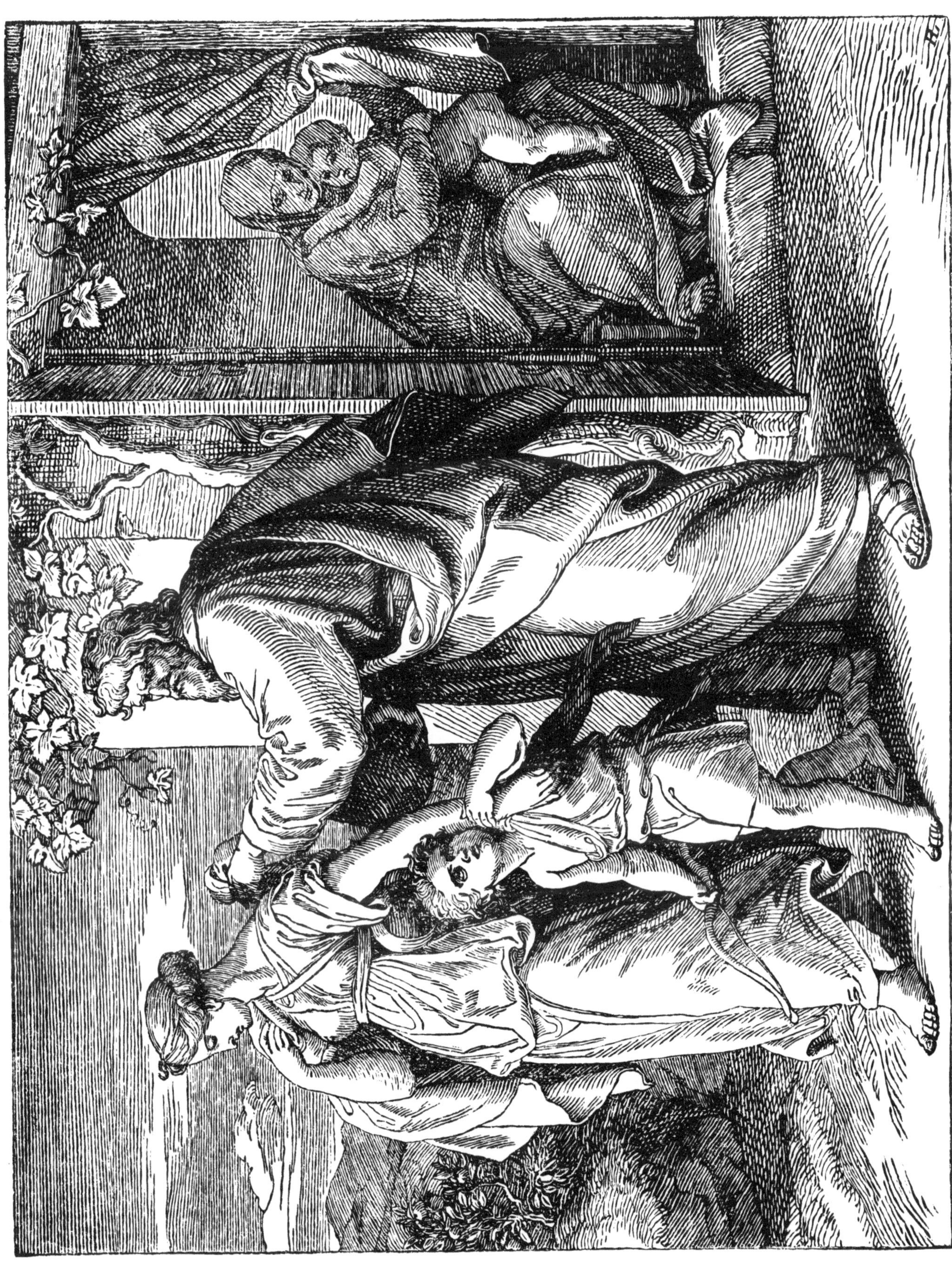

Departure of Hagar and Ishmael

The Lord gave to Abraham and Sarah a son, as he had promised, and Abraham called his name Isaac. Abraham was a hundred years old when Isaac was born.

And when Isaac grew to be a larger boy, Abraham made a great feast. Now Ishmael had thought that he should be his father's heir, and when he saw that he was supplanted, he was very angry, and spake bitter words, and would have done harm to the child. His mother also encouraged him in his misdoing. Then Sarah said to Abraham, cast out this bondwoman and her son; for the son of a bondwoman shall not be heir along with my son, even with Isaac. This was very grievous to Abraham, for he loved his son Ishmael. Then the Lord said to Abraham, Let not this thing that Sarah asketh be grievous unto thee. Hearken to her words, for indeed the blessing that I have promised to thee, and to thy children after thee, is not in Ishmael but in Isaac. Nevertheless, I will make of Ishmael a great nation.

Then Abraham believed that no harm should happen to the lad. Therefore he rose up early the next morning, and gave Hagar provision of bread and a bottle of water, putting it on her shoulder, and sent her and her son away.

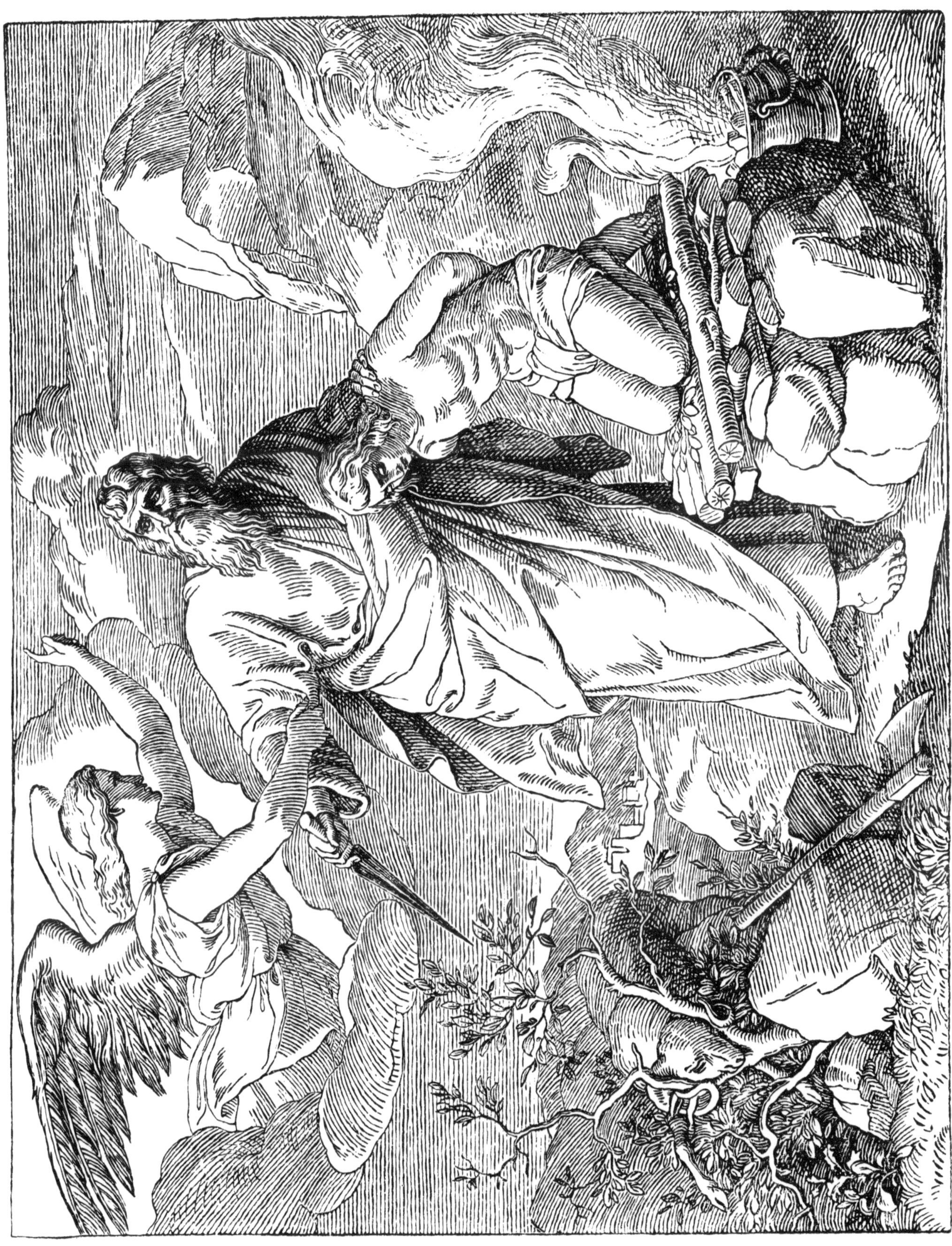

Abraham Offering Isaac

For many days did Abraham dwell in Beersheba, and he planted a grove there, and worshipped the Lord. After these things, God tried Abraham's faith, saying to him, Take now thy son, thine only son Isaac, whom thou lovest, and get thee into the land of Moriah, and offer him there for a burnt offering upon one of the mountains that I shall show thee.

So Abraham rose up early in the morning and saddled his donkey, and took two of his young men with him, and Isaac his son, and journeyed towards the place of which God had told him. He did not doubt but that the lad should come back again, even though he should slay him for a burnt offering, for he believed that the Lord would raise him up from the dead.

And he took wood for the burnt offering, and laid it upon Isaac; he took fire also, and a knife. And Isaac said to Abraham, Behold the fire and the wood; but where is the lamb for the burnt offering? And Abraham said, My son, God will provide Himself a lamb for a burnt offering. Then they came to the place of which God had told him; and Abraham built an altar there, and laid the wood in order, and bound Isaac, and laid him upon the wood.

Then he stretched forth his hand, and took the knife to slay his son. But the Angel of the Lord called to him out of heaven, and said, Abraham, Abraham! And he said, Here am I. Then the Lord said, Lay not thine hand on the lad, neither do thou anything unto him; for now I know that thou fearest God, seeing that thou hast not withheld thy son, thine only son, from me.

Then Abraham looked behind him, and saw a ram caught in the thicket by his horns, and he took the ram and offered it up for a sacrifice instead of Isaac his son.

Then the Lord spake again to him, saying, Because thou hast done this thing, and not withheld thy son from Me, I will bless thee, and I will multiply thy posterity as the stars of the heaven and as the sand of the seashore. And in thy posterity shall all the families of the earth be blessed, because thou hast obeyed my voice.

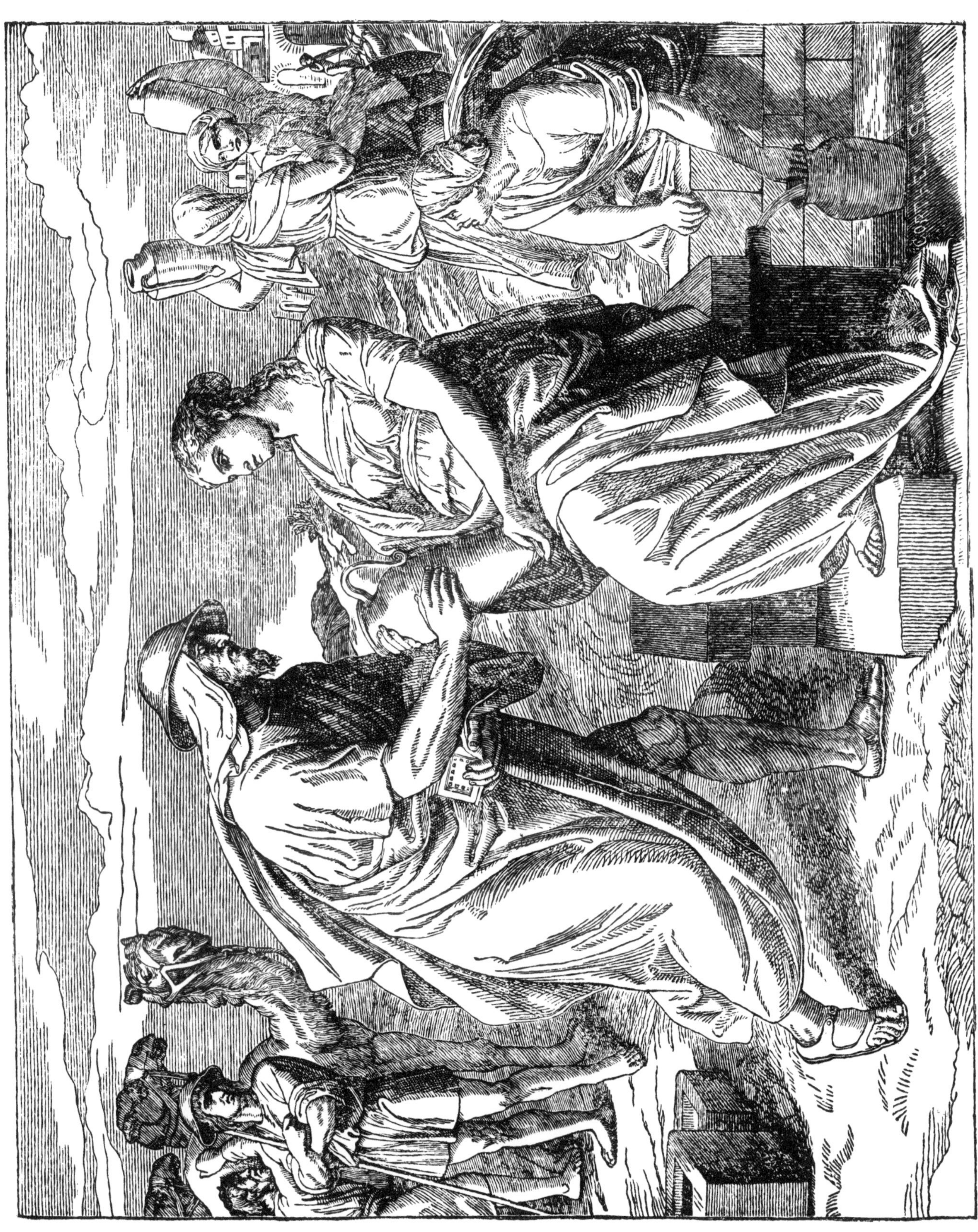

Abraham's Servant Meeting Rebekah

Abraham was now old, and it seemed good to him that he should find a wife for Isaac his son. So he spake to Eliezer of Damascus, the eldest servant of his house, and said, Thou shalt go unto my own kindred, and take a wife from among them for my son. Then Eliezer sware to his master that he would do his bidding. And he took ten camels of his master's — for all Abraham's goods were in his hand — and departed to Haran, in Mesopotamia, which was the city of Nahor.

And when he was come to the city, he made his camels kneel down by a well that was outside the walls; and it was evening, when the women go out to draw water. He prayed, saying, O Lord God of my master Abraham, I pray thee, show kindness to my master Abraham. Let this come to pass: if the damsel to whom I shall say, Let down thy pitcher that I may drink, shall say, Drink, and I will draw for thy camels also; let the same be she whom thou hast appointed for thy servant Isaac. Then shall I know that thou hast showed kindness to my master.

And while he was yet speaking, Rebekah came to the well. And she was a very fair virgin; and she went down to the well, and filled her pitcher, and came up again. Eliezer said to her, Let me, I pray thee, drink a little water out of thy pitcher. So she let down her pitcher from her shoulder, whereon she carried it, and gave him to drink. And when he had drunk, she said, I will draw for thy camels also, till they shall have done drinking. So she emptied the pitcher into the trough, and went down again to the well, and drew for all the camels. And the man held his peace, wondering whether or not the Lord had prospered his journey.

And he said to her, Whose daughter art thou? Is there room in thy father's house for us to lodge? She answered, I am the daughter of Bethuel, the son of Nahor. Then the man bowed down his head and worshipped, saying, Blessed be the Lord God of my master Abraham, for he hath not forgotten his mercy and truth, but hath led me to the house of my master's brethren.

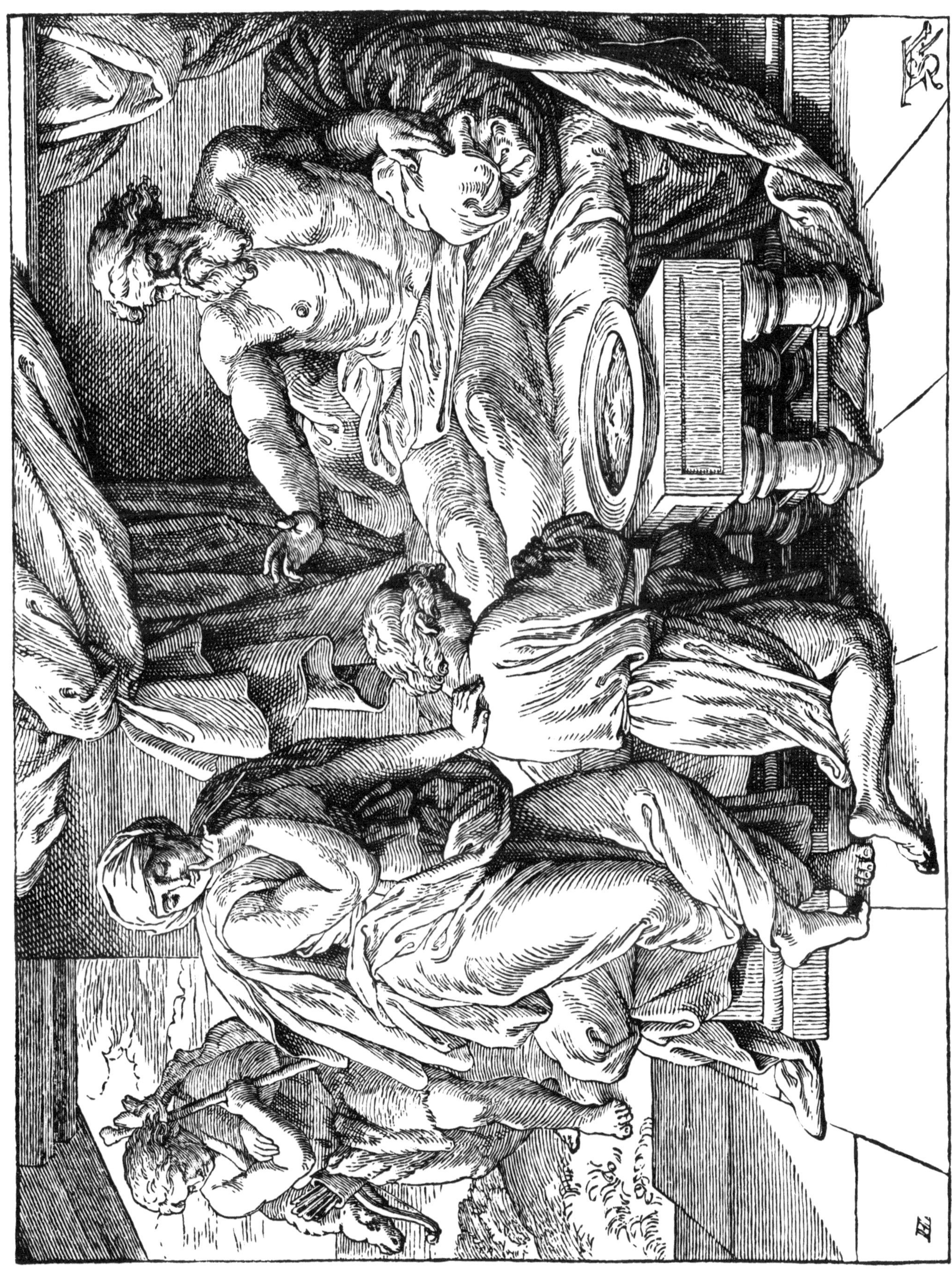

Isaac Blessing Jacob

Isaac and Rebekah, his wife, had two sons, named Esau and Jacob. Esau was a hunter, and Jacob was a shepherd. Isaac loved Esau because he had a taste for fresh game, but Rebekah loved Jacob. Esau was the elder of the two brothers, and as such, he had certain privileges called the birthright. The first-born son had twice as much of his father's goods as the other sons. When the father died, then he became the head of the family, and ruled over his brothers and sisters. But Esau did not care much for houses, land, silver and gold, and he sold his birthright to Jacob.

When Isaac was so old that he could not see, he called Esau to him and said: I am an old man and I know not how soon I may die. Take then thy quiver and thy bow, and go out into the field, and get me some venison. And make me a nice dish of it, such as I love, and bring it to me, that I may eat, and bless thee before I die.

And Rebekah heard when Isaac spoke to Esau; and Esau went to the field to hunt. And Rebekah told Jacob what Isaac had said to Esau. And she said, Now, my son, do as I command you. Go to the flock, and bring me two good kids from the goats, and I will season the meat well, and make such a dish as will please thy father. And thou shalt bring it to thy father, that he may eat, and bless *thee* before he dies.

Jacob said to Rebekah, But my brother Esau is a hairy man, and I am a smooth man. Perhaps my father will feel of me, and I shall seem to him as a deceiver, and I shall bring a curse upon myself, and not a blessing. His mother said, Upon me be thy curse my son. Do as I bid thee. And he went, and brought the young kids to his mother, and she made of them such a dish as his father loved.

And Rebekah took the best clothes of Esau and put them on Jacob. And she put the skins of the kids on his hands and his neck. And she gave the meat and the bread to Jacob. And he went to Isaac and said, My father. And Isaac said, Here am I; who art thou, my son? Jacob said, I am Esau thy first-born; I have done as thou didst bid me. Rise and eat of my venison, that thy soul may bless me.

Isaac said, How is it thou hast found it so quickly, my son? And he said, Because the Lord led the way. And Isaac said to Jacob, Come near that I may feel thee, whether thou be my son Esau. And Jacob went near to Isaac; and he felt him, and said, The voice is Jacob's voice, but the hands are the hands of Esau. And as he could not see, he blessed him, thinking he was Esau. And he said, Art thou my very son Esau? And Jacob said, I am. And Isaac told his son that God would take care of him, and give him great wealth, and make him a ruler over many nations.

Jacob had scarcely left the presence of Isaac, when Esau came in from the hunt. And he also cooked meat and brought it to his father, and said, Rise now, and eat of thy son's venison, that thy soul may bless me. And Isaac said to him, Who art thou? And he said, I am thy first-born, Esau. And Isaac trembled greatly, and said, Who and where is he that hath taken venison, and brought it to me, and I have eaten before thou camest, and have blessed him? Yea, and he shall be blessed.

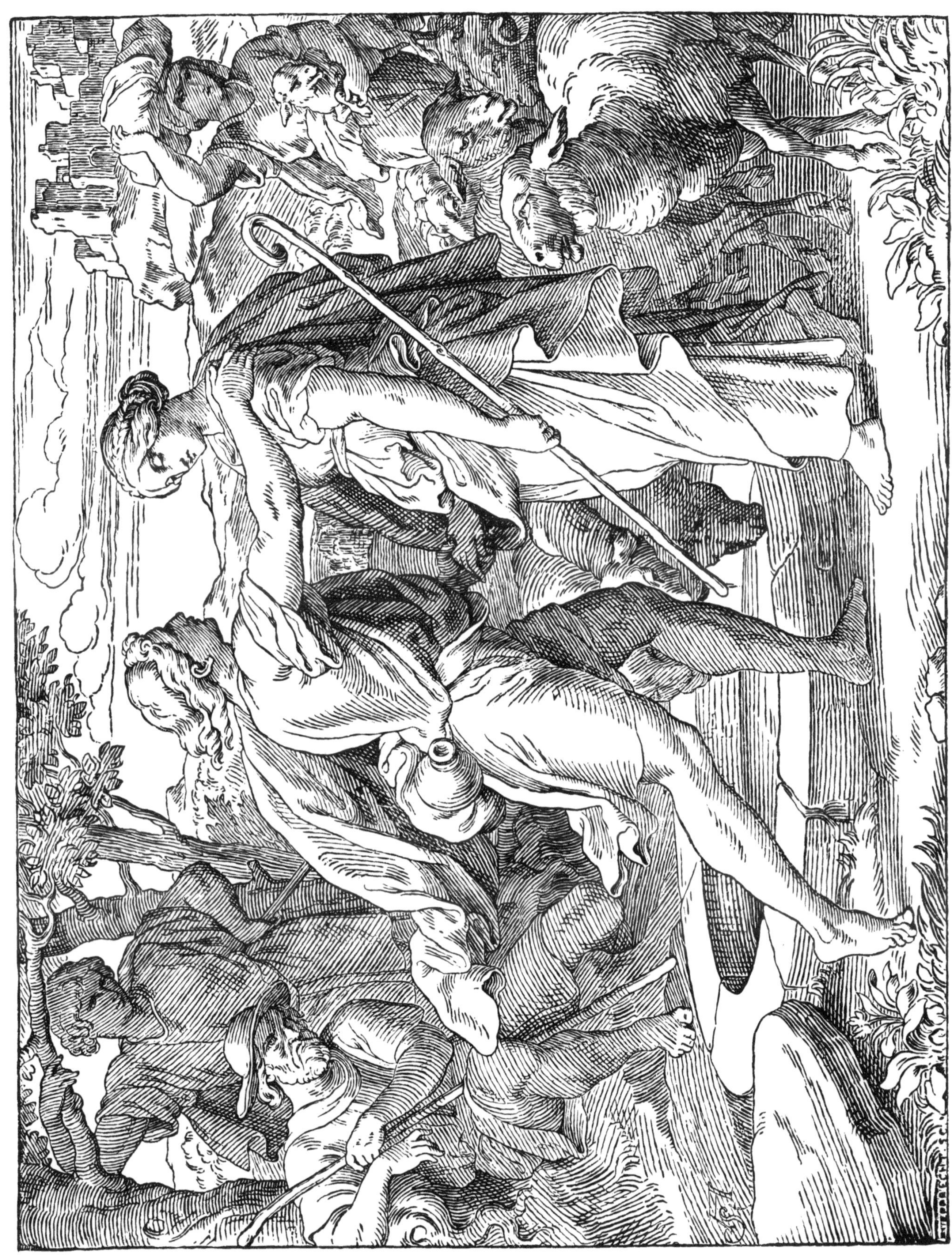

Jacob Meeting Rachel

Esau hated his brother Jacob because of the blessing his father had given him; and he planned to kill his brother as soon as his father was laid in the grave. Rebekah, their mother, sent for Jacob, and told him that Esau meant to kill him, and bade him go to Haran, where Laban, her brother, dwelt, and stay with him till Esau's anger was turned away. And Rebekah made an excuse to Isaac for sending her favorite son away. She was not pleased with Esau's wives, nor did she wish her son Jacob to take a wife from the daughters of Heth. She told Isaac so, and Isaac sent Jacob to take a wife from among the daughters of Laban, the brother of Rebekah.

Then Jacob went on his journey, and took his way toward Haran. And he looked, and saw shepherds, and a well in a field; and lo, there were three flocks of sheep lying by it; for out of that well they watered the flocks. And Jacob drew near and asked them whence they came. We are from Haran, they said. Do you know Laban, the son of Nahor? inquired Jacob. And they said, We know him. Jacob said to them, Is he well? They said, He is well.

And while he yet spake with them, Rachel came up with her father's sheep, for she took care of them. And when Jacob saw Rachel, he drew near, and rolled the stone from the mouth of the well, and watered the flock of Laban, his mother's brother. And Jacob kissed Rachel and wept for joy. And he told her that her father was his uncle, and that he was Rebekah's son.

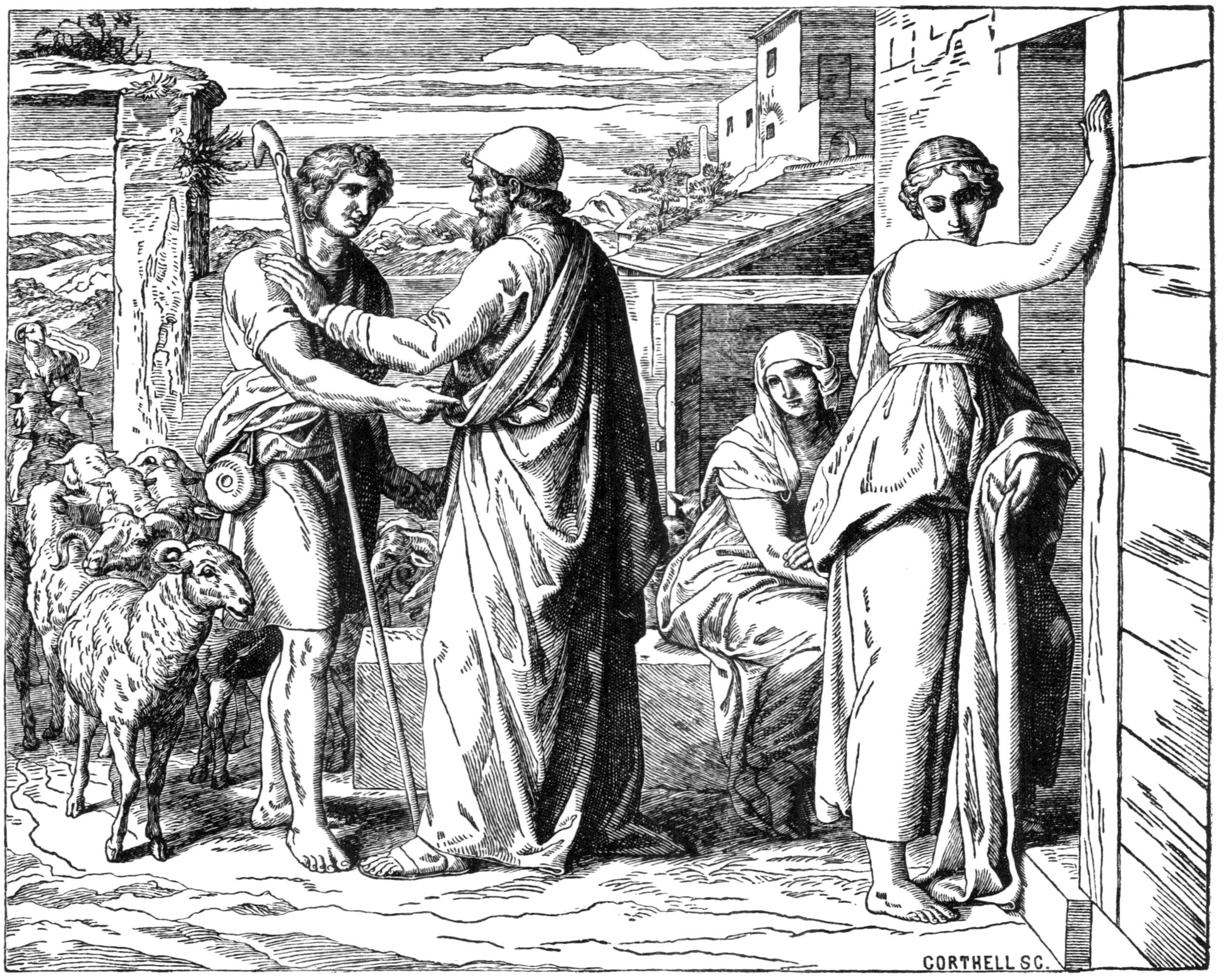
CORTHELL SC.

Laban Hiring Jacob

Jacob had worked for his uncle Laban for a month; then Laban said to Jacob, Because thou art related to me, shouldst thou work for me for nothing? Tell me what shall thy wages be?

Laban had two daughters: the name of the elder was Leah, and the name of the younger was Rachel. Leah was tender-eyed, but Rachel was beautiful and well formed. And Jacob loved Rachel. So when Laban asked what wages he would take, he said, I will serve thee seven years for Rachel, thy younger daughter. Laban said, It is better that I give her to thee, than that I should give her to another man. So stay with me. And Jacob served seven years for Rachel, and they seemed to him but a few days, so great was his love for her.

And Jacob said to Laban, Give me my wife, for the time is up that I said I would serve thee. And Laban gathered together all the men of the place and made a feast. And in the evening he brought in Leah, closely veiled, so that her face could not be seen, and Jacob took her for his wife. In the morning Jacob saw that it was Leah whom he had wed; and he went at once to Laban, and said, What is this thou hast done to me? Did I not serve with thee for Rachel? Why hast thou played me such a trick?

Laban said, It is not the custom of our country to give the younger before the first-born. Be true to Leah, and thou shalt have Rachel also, if thou wilt serve me for another seven years. And Jacob did so, and Laban gave him his daughter Rachel for a wife, for there was no law in those days to prevent a man from having more than one wife. And Jacob loved Rachel far more than he did Leah, and stayed with Laban even another seven years on her account.

God gave children to Leah; but Rachel had no children, and her heart was sad, and she was very jealous of her sister. But at last God heard her prayer, and gave Rachel a son. And she called his name Joseph.

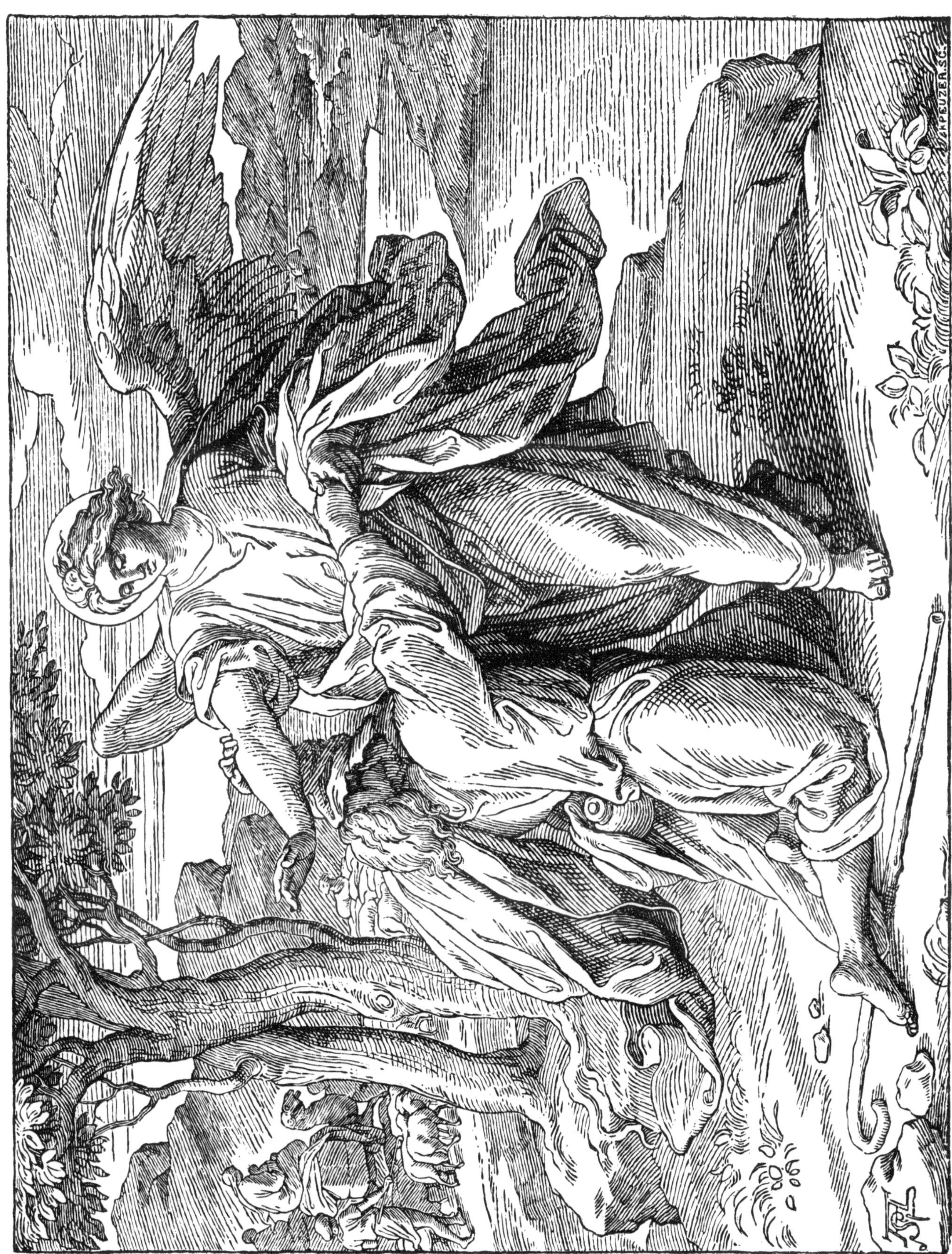

Jacob Wrestling with the Angel

Jacob had become a rich man, and had flocks and herds of his own, and Laban's son spoke ill of Jacob; and Laban was not the good friend to him that he had been. And God told Jacob to go back to his own country. So Jacob put his wives and his sons on camels, and took all the flocks and herds, and everything that he owned, and left Laban, and went back to the home of Isaac, his father. And on the way a company of angels met him. And when Jacob saw them he said, This is God's host.

Jacob was still afraid of his brother Esau, and had sent messengers to speak with him, and to offer him rich gifts if he would be at peace with him. The messengers brought word that Esau was on his way to meet Jacob with four hundred men. Jacob was in great fear, and prayed to God to save him from the hands of his brother who hated him so. He said, I am not worthy the least of thy mercies, and of all the kind care thou hast given me. But save me, I pray thee, from the hand of my brother Esau, for I fear him, lest he will come and smite me.

One night Jacob was left alone, and there came an angel, who wrestled with him till the break of day. And when the angel saw that he could not throw Jacob, he touched the hollow of his thigh and put it out of joint. And he said, Let me go, for the day breaketh. And Jacob said, I will not let thee go, except thou bless me. And the angel said to him, What is thy name? And he said, Jacob. The angel said, Thy name shall be called no more Jacob, but Israel: for as a prince thou hast power with God and with men. The word Israel means, A Prince of God.

And Jacob said to the angel, who was in the form of a man, Tell me, I pray thee, thy name. And he said, Why dost thou need to ask my name? And he blessed him then and there. And Jacob called the name of the place Peniel, which means The Face of God: for I have seen God face to face, and my life is saved.

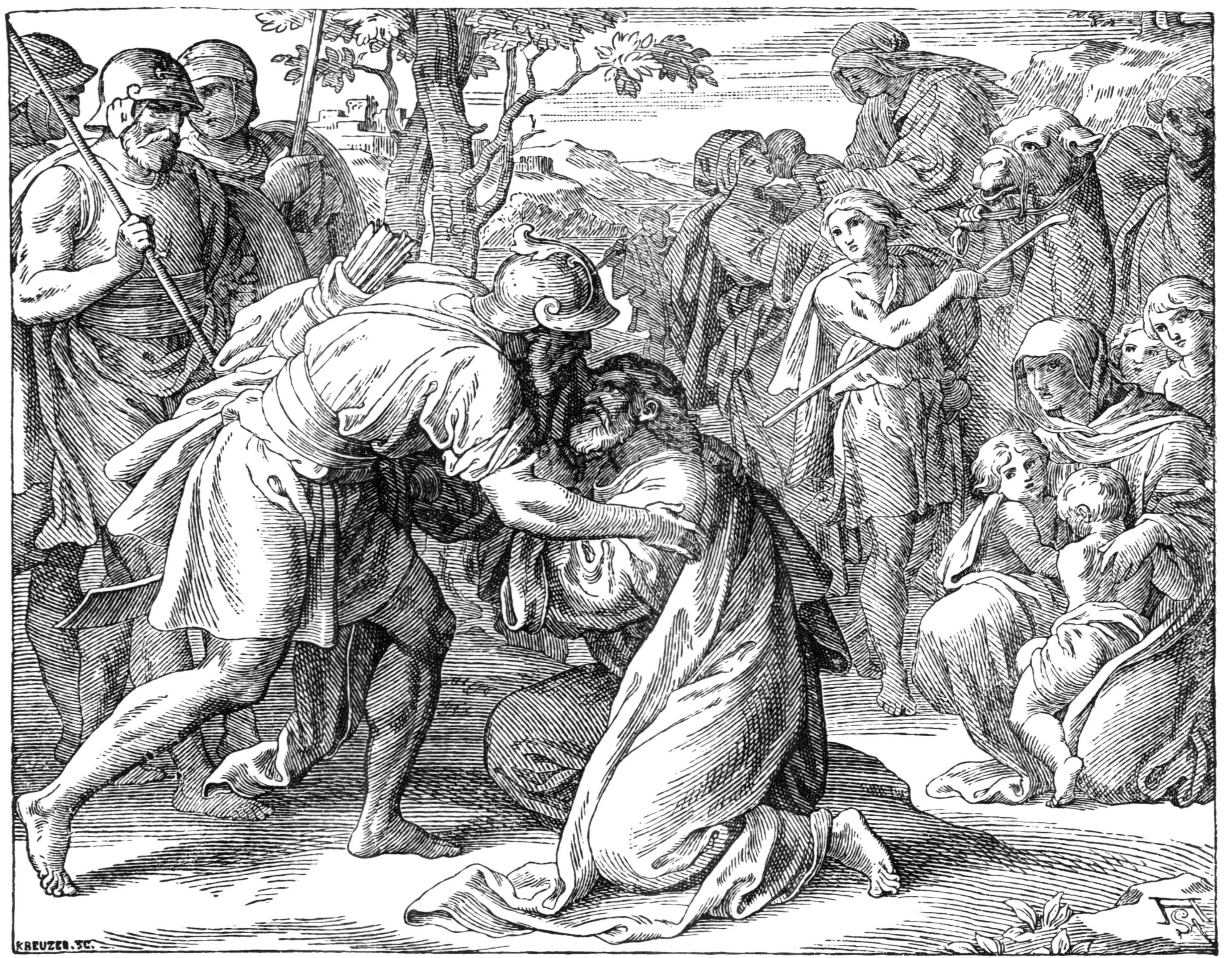
KREUZER. SC.

Meeting of Jacob and Esau

Jacob saw Esau coming with his four hundred men. And he went out in front of his wives and children, and bowed down to the ground seven times on his way to his brother. And Esau ran to meet him, and fell on his neck and kissed him; and they both wept together, and all the past was forgiven. Then Esau raised his eyes, and saw the women and children, and said, Who are those with thee? And Jacob said, The children which God hath given thy servant. And they all bowed down before Esau. Then Esau said, What meanest thou by all this drove which I met? Jacob told him they were sent as a present to him. Esau said, I have enough, my brother; keep what is thine own.

And Jacob said, Nay, I pray thee, if now I have found grace in thy sight, then take the present I bring. For to have seen thy face, and to know thou art pleased with me, is as if I had seen the face of God. He said God had been good to him, and he had enough and to spare, and he urged Esau so strongly to take his gifts, that Esau did so. And Esau went back to Seir, where he lived; and Jacob went on his way. And God told him to go up to Bethel and dwell there for a while, and build there an altar to the God who came to him when he fled from his brother Esau.

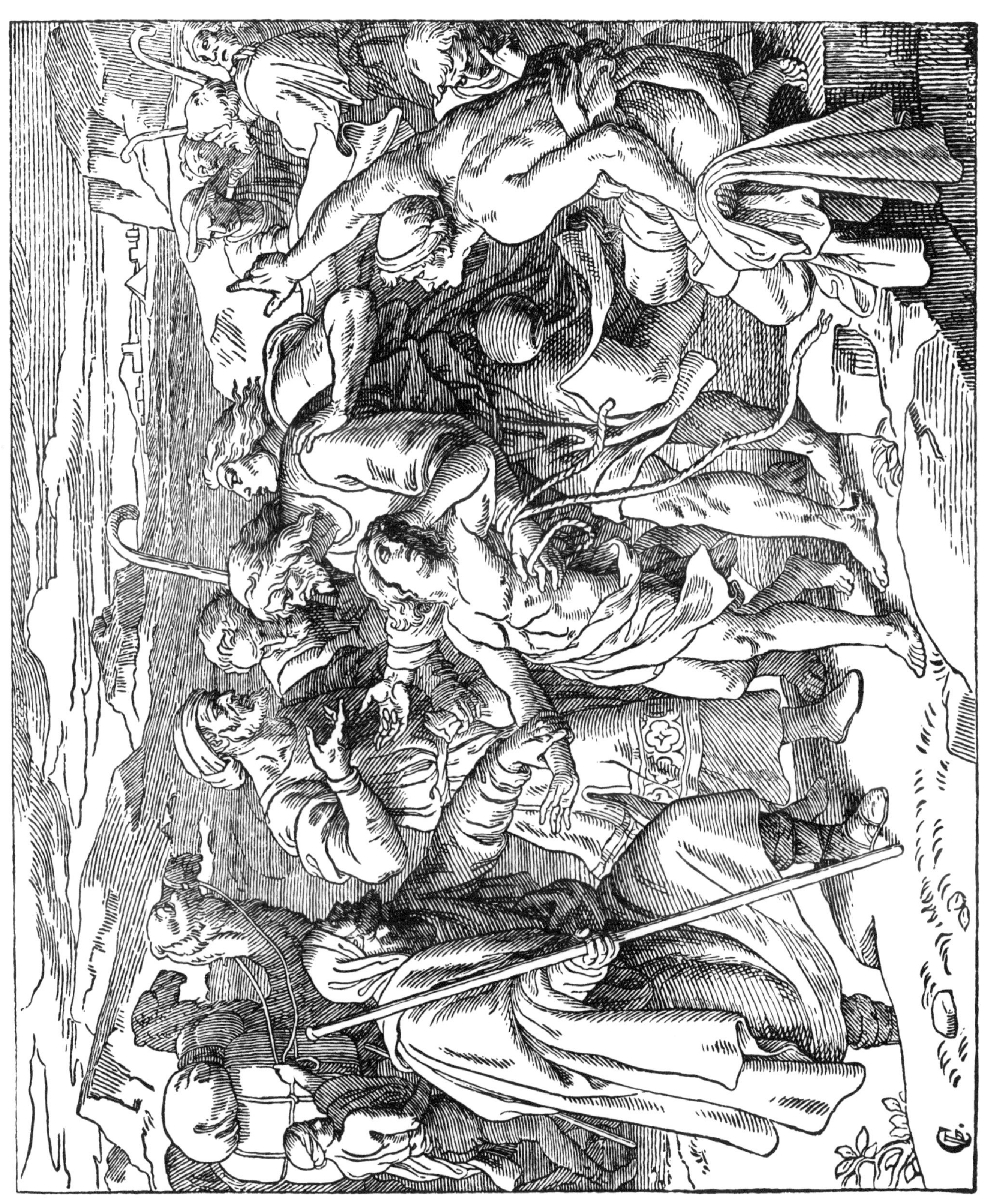

Joseph Sold by his Brethren

Jacob had twelve sons. The youngest two were Joseph and Benjamin, whose mother was Rachel. Jacob's sons were shepherds; and Joseph too, as soon as he was old enough, was sent out into the fields to help his brothers to feed the flocks. Now of all his sons, Jacob loved Joseph the most. He was the child of Rachel whom Jacob dearly loved; and also Joseph was more upright and true than his elder brothers. When he was with them out in the fields he saw them doing many wrong things, and he thought their father ought to know it. So Joseph told him of all their wicked conduct, and this made them dislike him very much. Besides this, they had another reason for hating him. Their father Jacob, to show how much he loved his favorite son, gave him a coat of many colors. This was a mark of great distinction and honor, and it is supposed also to have been a sign that the person wearing it was intended to be his father's heir. All these things made Joseph's brothers so angry and jealous that they could not speak peaceably to him; they hated him, and were rough and unkind to him.

After a time, Joseph's brothers took their father's flock to Shechem to feed them there. One day Jacob said to Joseph, Your brothers are feeding the flock in Shechem. Come, and I will send you to them. See whether it be well with your brothers, and well with the flocks; and bring me word again.

So Joseph went after his brothers, but while he was still a long way off, his brothers saw him as he was crossing the valley to meet them; and at the sight of him, wearing the coat of many colors, all their bitter, jealous feelings grew more strong. And after Joseph had arrived, the brothers saw a company of Ishmaelites, with their camels, coming their way. And when the Ishmaelites passed by, they sold Joseph to them for twenty pieces of silver. And the Ishmaelites took him, and carried him into Egypt to be a slave.

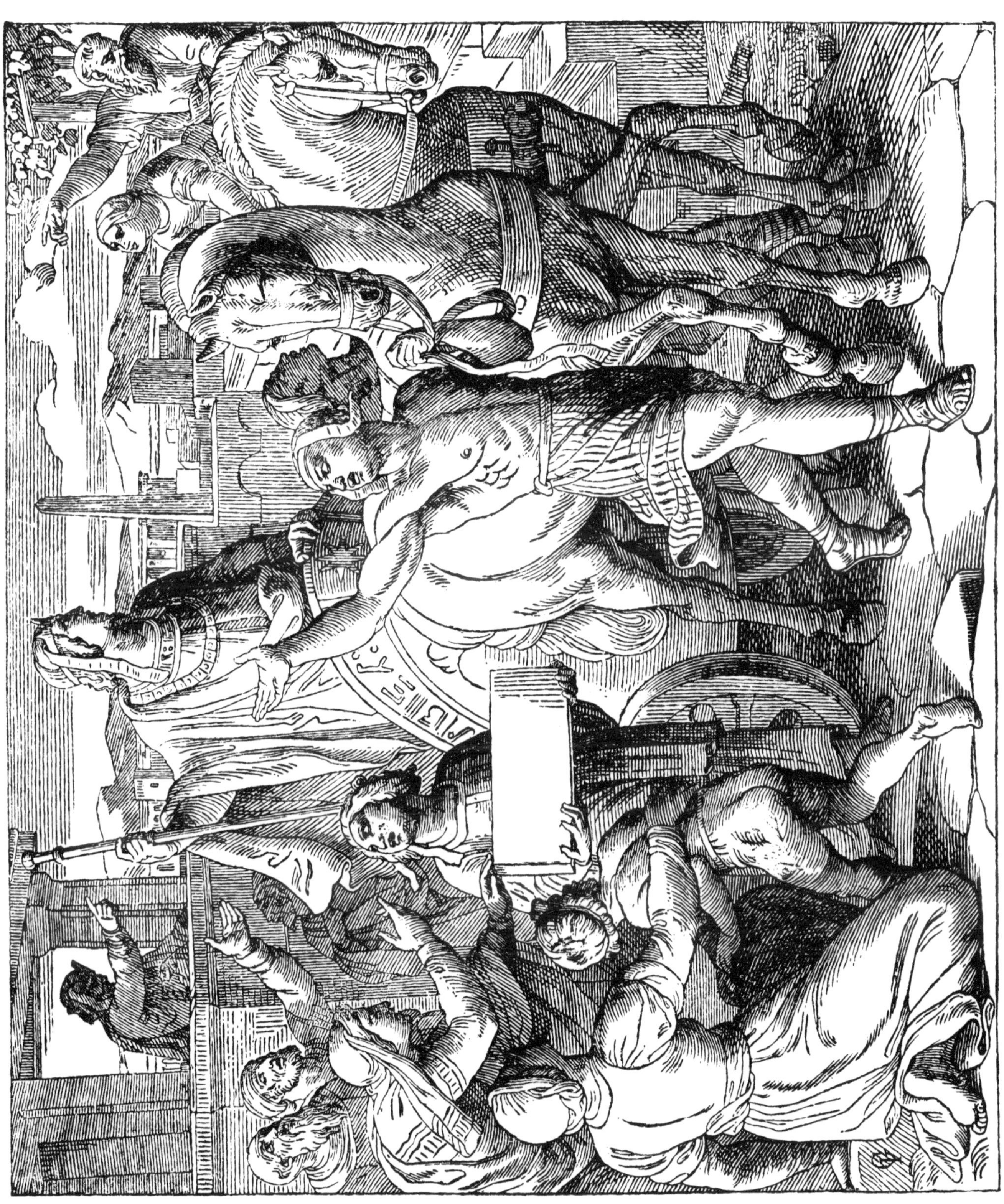

Joseph Proclaimed Ruler of Egypt

One night Pharaoh, king of Egypt, had a very strange dream and his spirit was troubled; but none of the wise men of Egypt could tell him the meaning. The servants of Pharoah knew that Joseph was able to explain the meaning of dreams. When Pharaoh heard this, he ordered some men to bring Joseph to him.

Pharaoh told Joseph his dreams. And Joseph said God has showed Pharaoh what he is going to do. There are going to be seven years of plenty in all the land of Egypt. But afterwards there will come seven years of famine.

When Joseph had finished explaining about the dreams to Pharaoh, he began to advise the king what to do. He said, Let Pharaoh find a man who is very prudent and wise, and let him be set over the land of Egypt. And while the seven years of plenty last, let him be careful to gather up all the food of those good years, and save up corn for Pharaoh. So, when the seven years of famine come, there will be food for the people; and the land will not be destroyed with famine, even though no corn will be growing in the fields.

And Pharaoh said to his servants, Where can we find such a wise man as Joseph? for the Spirit of God is in him. And Pharaoh said unto Joseph, Because God has showed you all this, I know that you are more wise and prudent than anyone else. So I will set you over my house, and all my people shall be ruled as you advise. And you shall be greater than any other man in my kingdom, except myself.

And Pharaoh took off his ring from his hand, and put it upon Joseph's hand; and he gave him beautiful garments to wear, and he put a gold chain round his neck. He also made him to ride in a very grand chariot — one of his own carriages — and they called him the Father of the country.

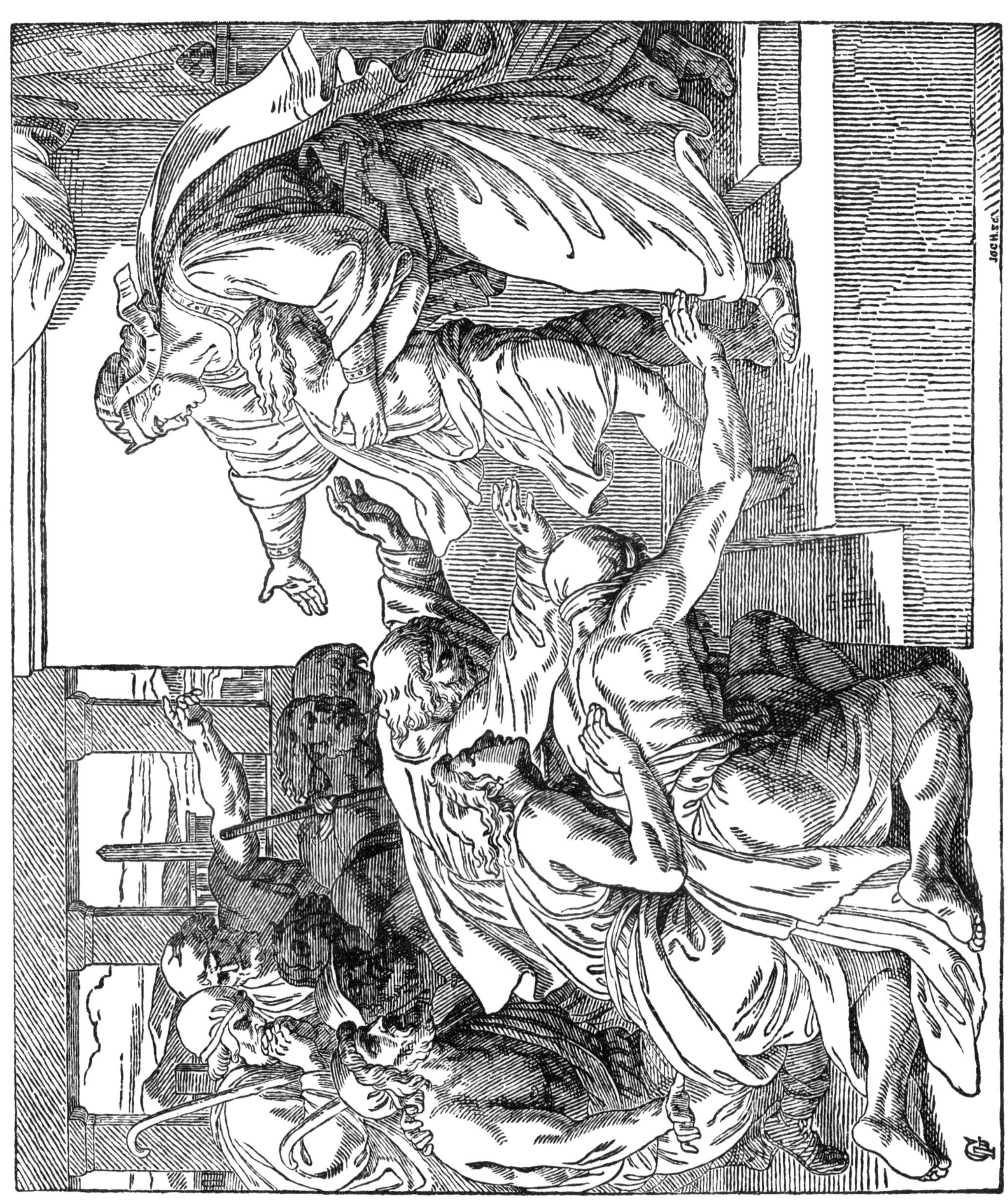

Joseph Makes Himself Known to his Brethren

The famine, which Joseph had predicted, came upon Egypt and upon Canaan after the seven years of plenty ended. However, in the land of Egypt there was grain stored up in abundance because of the grace and wisdom which God gave to Joseph.

When Jacob heard that Egypt had grain, he sent Joseph's ten older brothers to buy some. But he did not send Benjamin, Joseph's younger brother, for fear that harm would come to him. Joseph recognized his older brothers, but they did not recognize him, because they had not seen him for more than twenty years and, in their minds, Joseph was dead.

Joseph did not immediately reveal himself to his brothers, because he wanted to test them first, to know whether their wicked hearts had changed. Joseph asked them many questions, he spoke harshly, accused them of being spies and locked them in prison. He wanted to make them think about their lives and the condition of their hearts before God. Three days later, Joseph allowed them to depart, but kept one of them in prison, telling the others to return to Egypt.

And after many months, the older brothers returned to Egypt to buy more grain. This time, Joseph made himself known. He could not keep back his tears as he said to his brethren, I am Joseph; does my father yet live? And his brethren could not answer him, for they were terrified at his presence. He saw how afraid they were, and that because of their great surprise and fear, they had not a word to say; so he spoke to them most lovingly. Come near to me, he said, and they came near. Then he said to them, I am Joseph your brother, whom you sold into Egypt. Now therefore be not grieved nor angry with yourselves that you sold me; for it was God's doing. He sent me before you to preserve life, that people should not die of starvation. For two years there has been famine in the land, and yet there are five more years to come, during which there shall be no ploughing nor harvest, for no corn will grow. And God sent me before you to save food, that your lives might be saved by a great deliverance.

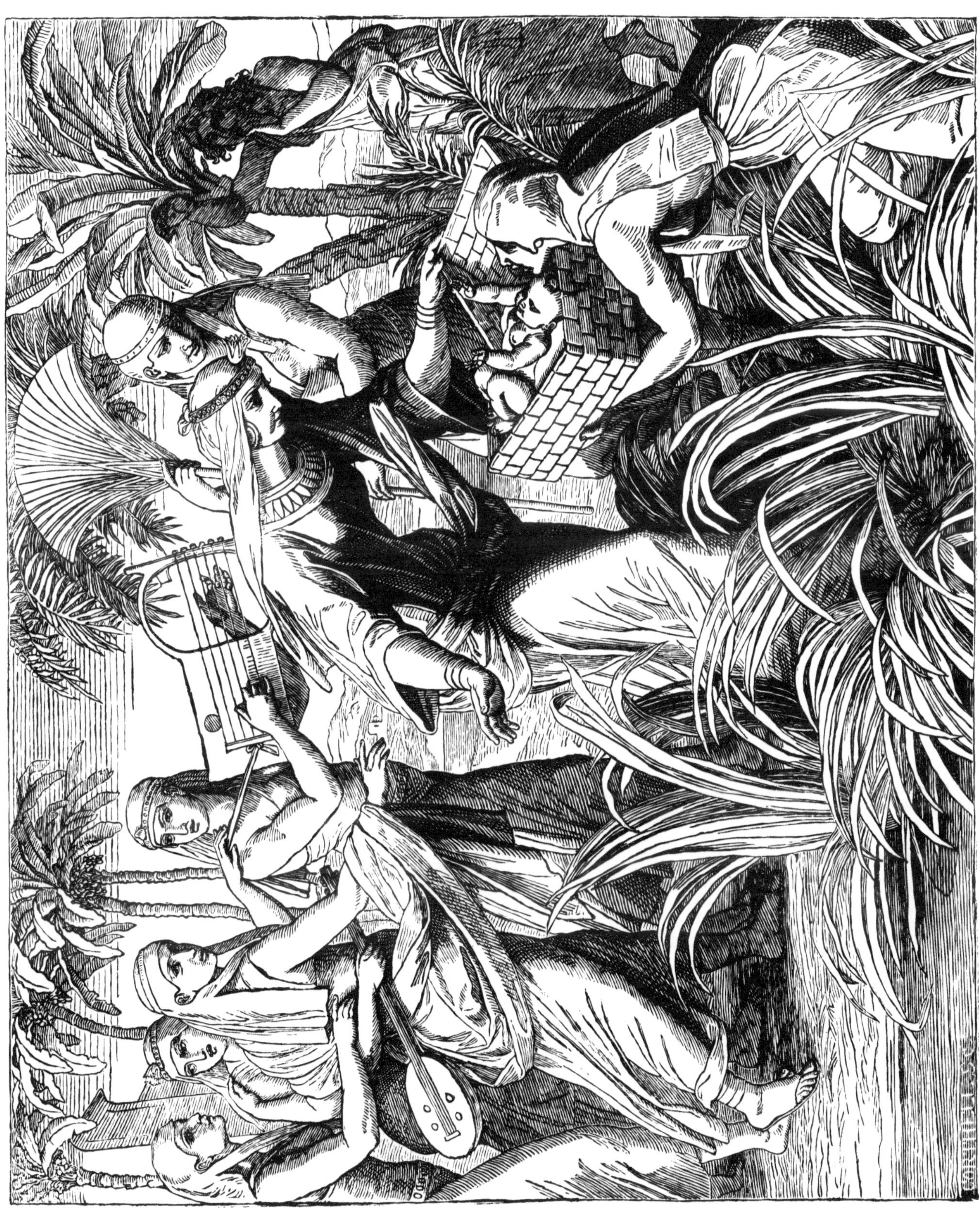

PHARAOH'S DAUGHER FINDING MOSES

Pharaoh, the king of Egypt, did not like to see the families of the children of Israel becoming so large, and living in the best part of Egypt. So he told the nurses who went to help the mothers take care of their little children, to throw all the boy babies into the river Nile as soon as they were born. The nurses did not obey this wicked law, but saved all the babies that they could.

At this time there lived a good man and his wife, who had one daughter named Miriam, and a little boy three years old, named Aaron. He was born before the king made this cruel law. Then another child was born; it was a little boy. He was such a beautiful baby that the mother said, I cannot throw him into the river.

For three months she took great pains to hide him, so that the Egyptians should not know that she had a little child. At the end of that time she could hide him no longer, for he was bigger and cried louder; and she was sadly afraid that he would be discovered. She soon thought of what she would do.

The mother thought. I will make a cradle-boat for my baby to lie in when I put him into the river. So she took papyrus leaves, and plaited them into a cradle. When this little boat was made, she covered it on the outside with pitch, so as to keep the water out.

The mother with many tears and prayers lifted the child from her bosom, and laid him in this cradle. Then she carried it to the river, and placed it among the tall rushes which grew on its banks. She dared not stop to watch it herself, but she told her daughter Miriam to stay near the place, and see what became of it.

Soon Miriam saw a lady and her maids coming along. She was a princess, the daughter of Pharaoh the king. As she passed by the riverside, the lady saw something like a tiny boat among the rushes. She told one of her maids to draw it out and bring it to her.

When she opened it, she saw in it a lovely babe. As she and her maid looked, the child cried. The princess felt sorry for the poor little one; she knew that it was one of the Hebrew children that had been put there, so that it might not be killed according to her father's order. This beautiful boy shall be my child, she said; I will take care of him.

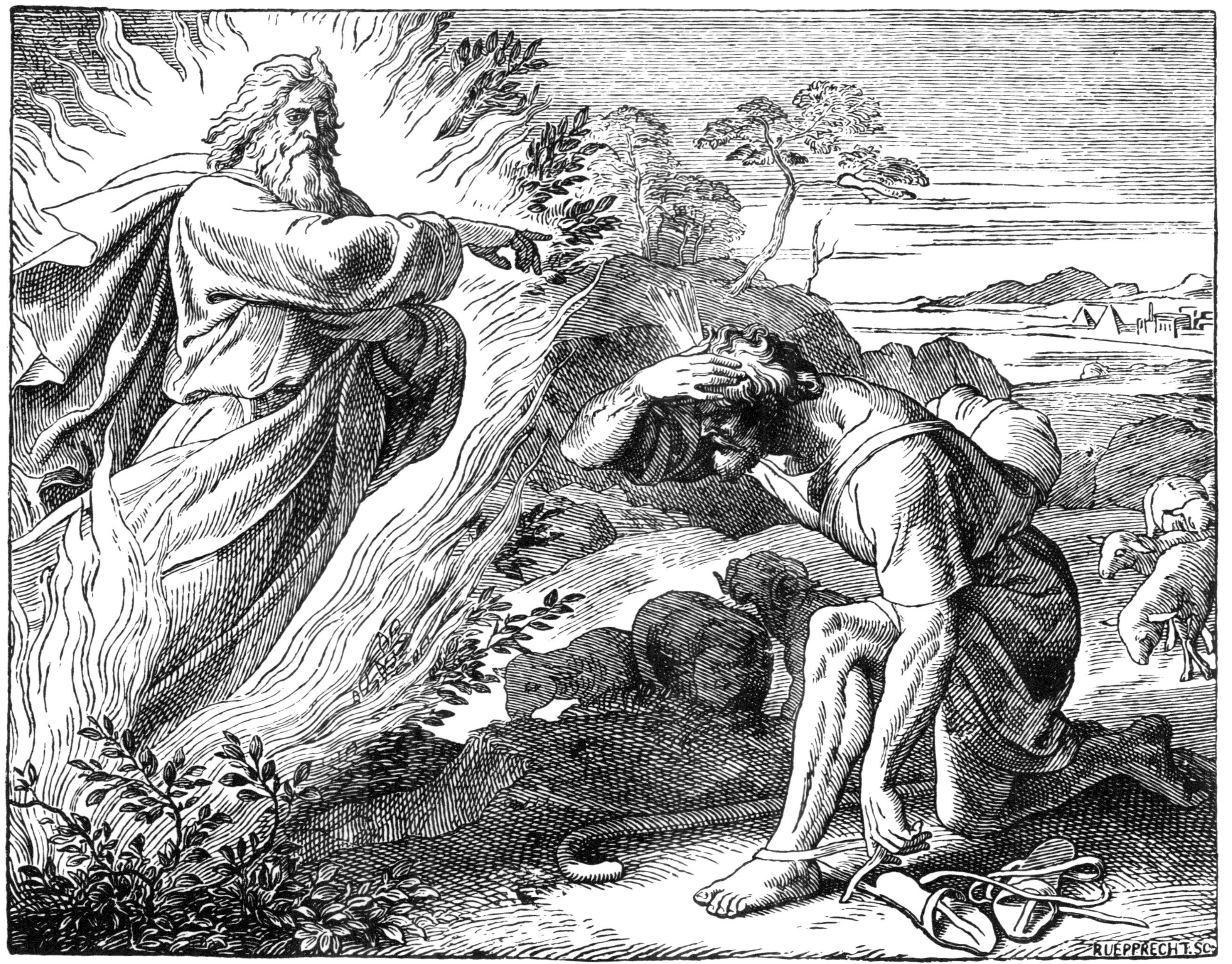
RUEPPRECHT. SC.

Moses at the Burning Bush

Now Moses kept the flock of Jethro his father-in-law, the priest of Midian; and on a certain occasion he drove his flock into the inner part of the desert, and came to the mountain of God on his way towards Horeb. And the Angel of the Lord appeared unto him in a flame of fire out of the midst of a bush; and he looked, and, behold, the bush burned with fire, but was not consumed. And Moses said, I will go and see this great sight, why the bush is not burnt.

And when the Lord saw that he went forward, He called to him out of the midst of the bush and said. Moses, Moses. And he answered, Here I am. And he said, Come not nigh hither, put off thy shoes from thy feet, for the place whereon thou standest is holy ground; I am the God of thy father, the God of Abraham, the God of Isaac and the God of Jacob. And Moses hid his face, for he was afraid to look upon God.

And the Lord said to him, I have surely seen the affliction of my people in Egypt and I have heard their cry by reason of their taskmasters; for I know their sorrows. And I am come down to deliver them out of the hand of the Egyptians, and to bring them out of that land into a good and large land, into a land flowing with milk and honey. Come now therefore, and I will send thee to Pharaoh, that thou mayest bring forth my people, the children of Israel, out of Egypt.

But Moses said unto God, Who am I, that I should go to Pharaoh? And that I should bring forth the children of Israel out of Egypt? God answered, Certainly I will be with thee, and thus shalt thou say to the children of Israel, Jehovah, the God of your fathers, hath sent me unto you.

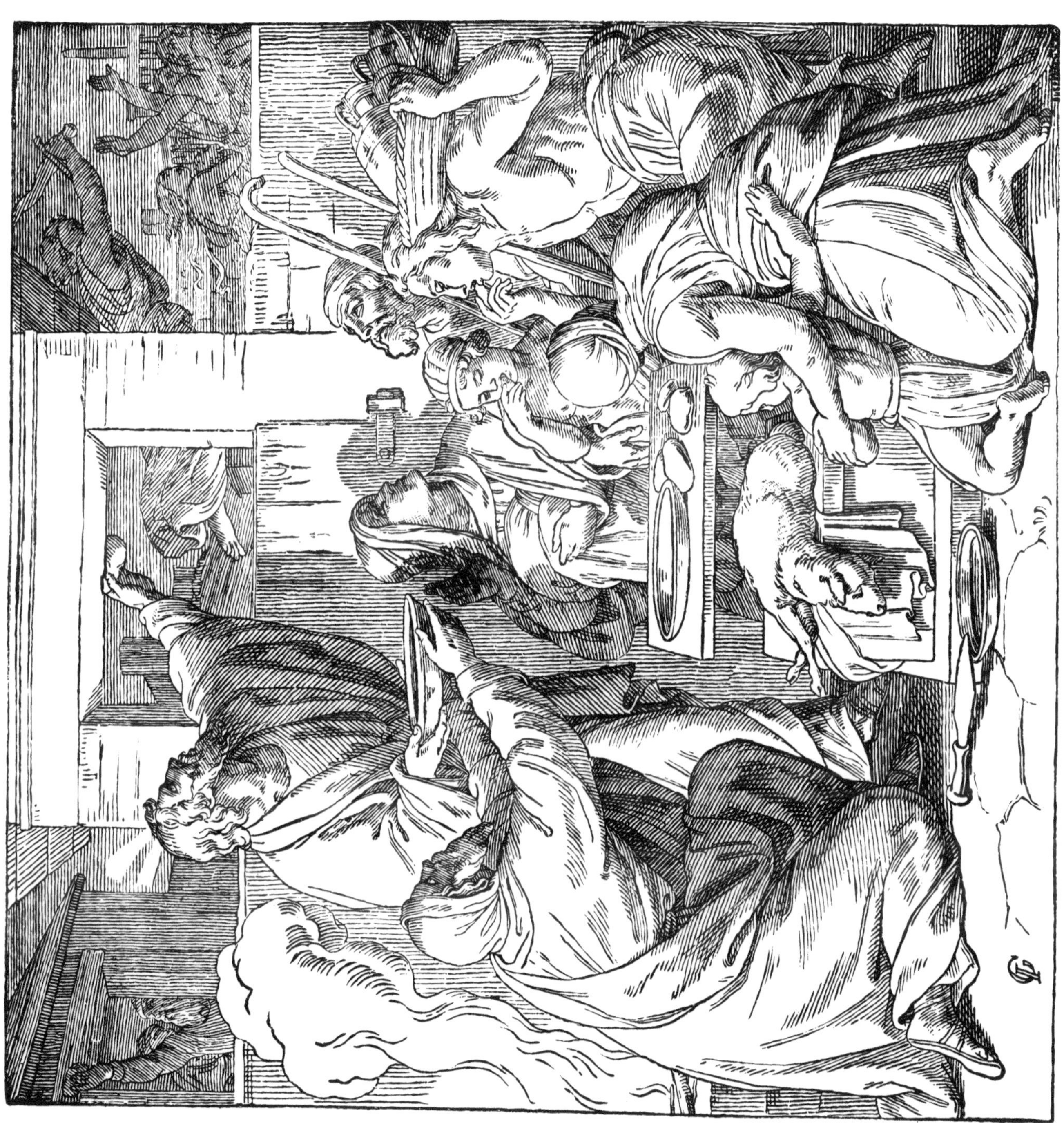

The Feast of the Passover

The Children of Israel had been enslaved in Egypt by Pharoah for many generations of oppression when God spoke to Moses and instructed him to go to Pharoah to let God's people go free. Pharoah refused, and Moses, acting as God's messenger, brought down a series of 10 plagues on Egypt. The last plague was the slaying of the firstborn.

Moses had told the Israelites to prepare for a journey, for on that very night God would make Pharaoh consent to let them go. God had said, Tell them, I will pass through the land of Egypt, about midnight, and all the firstborn, both of man and beast, in the land of Egypt shall die; but I will pass over your houses and not smite your firstborn. You must kill a lamb and sprinkle its blood on your doorposts: then, when I see the blood, I will pass over you, and the plague shall not destroy you. You must stay indoors that night and eat a feast while the Lord is passing through the land to destroy the Egyptians, This feast is to be called the feast of the Passover and you must keep it every year as the day comes round. They were to eat with their shoes on their feet, with their staves in their hands, and to eat in haste, so as to be ready at a moment's notice when the order came to start on their journey.

While the Israelites were thus eating that Passover feast, the order came for them all at once to leave the land of Egypt, where they had lived so many years. They were quite ready to go; not one moment did they wait; and the Egyptians, who before were so anxious to keep them, now almost thrust them out of their land. This going out of the Israelites from Egypt is called the Exodus — which means departure.

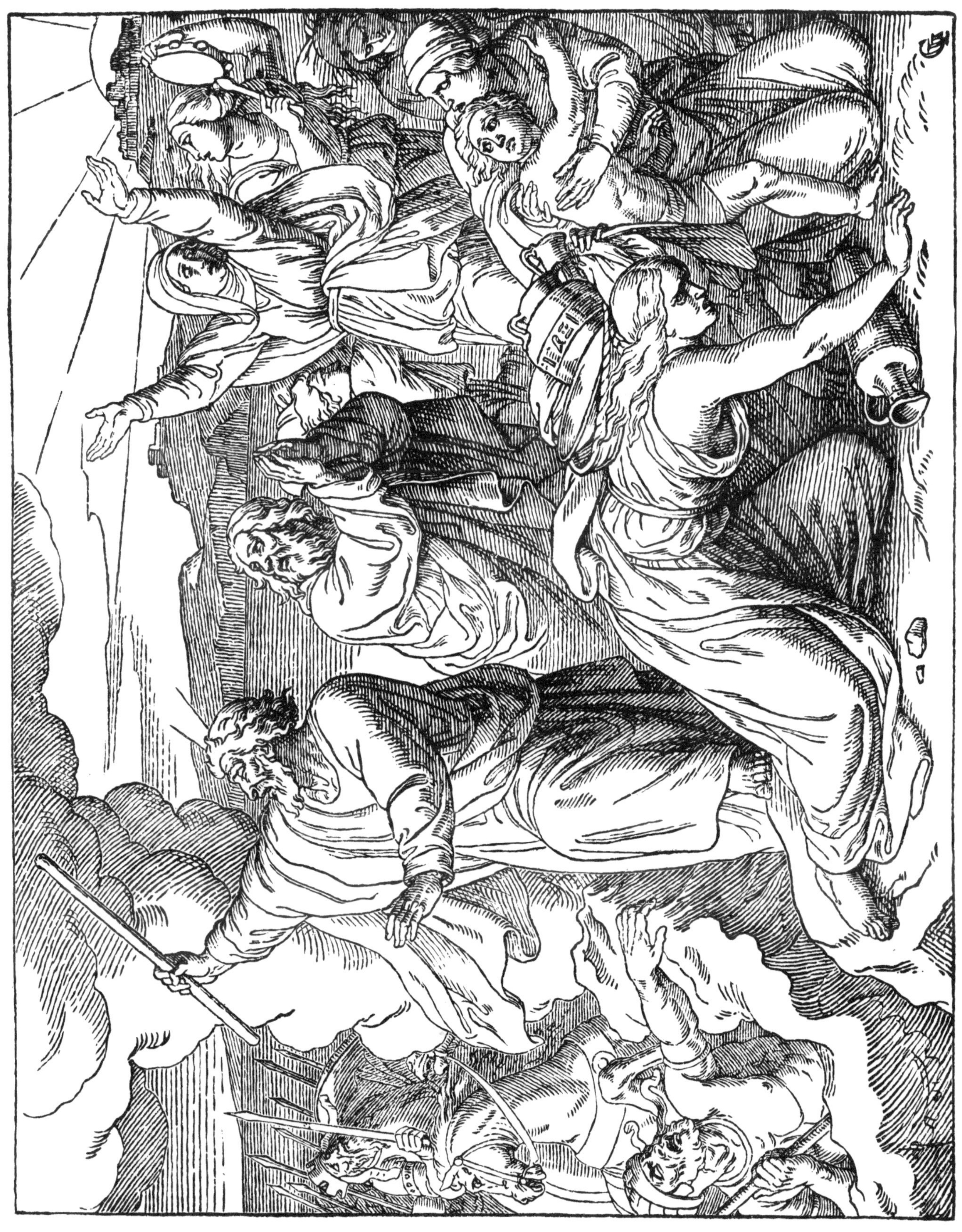

Pharaoh's Host Destroyed in the Red Sea

Soon after the exodus of the Israelites from Egypt, Pharaoh and his servants said, Why did we let the Israelites go from serving us? What shall we do without their labor? Let us go and make them come back to their work. So they made ready all the horses and chariots of Pharaoh, and overtook the Israelites as they were camped by the sea. Great was the terror of the Israelites as they saw these armed men coming towards them. They had no arms themselves, so they could not fight them. They were shut in by the mountains on the one side, and by the Red Sea on the other, so they could not run away from them. There seemed no way in which they could get out of their hands.

In their distress they cried to God and he heard them. He said, You can do nothing, you need do nothing; I will do all. Fear not, stand still, and see the salvation of God; for the Egyptians whom ye have seen today, ye shall see again no more for ever.

The Israelites were trembling with fear, when all at once they saw a pillar of fire move through the air and come between them and the Egyptians. It was a pillar of fire and a pillar of cloud both at once. To them it was a pillar of fire giving them light, but to the Egyptians it was a pillar of cloud, covering them with darkness. The Egyptians could not see the camp of the Israelites all night, for the thick cloud hid them from sight. Still they thought that they were safe in their power; they could not climb the mountains and they could not walk over the sea.

Then Moses, at the command of God, stretched out his rod over the waters of the Red Sea, and they divided, and the sea was like a wall on the right hand and on the left. And a strong wind dried up a pathway for them through the sea. Now, Moses said, Go forward; so this vast host began its journey through this wonderful road to the land on the opposite side. It is supposed that the sea was eight miles wide in that part where the Israelites crossed.

When the Egyptians came to the spot where they thought the Israelites were staying, they found them gone. And the Egyptians went after them to the sea, even all of Pharaoh's horses, chariots, and horsemen. And it came to pass, that the Lord looked unto the host of the Egyptians and troubled them, and took off their chariot wheels, that they drave them heavily: so that the Egyptians said, Let us flee from the face of Israel; for the Lord fighteth for them against the Egyptians. And the Lord said unto Moses, Stretch out thine hand over the sea, that the waters may come again upon the Egyptians. And Moses stretched forth his hand over the sea, and the sea returned to his strength; and the Egyptians fled against it; and the Lord overthrew the Egyptians in the midst of the sea. And the waters returned, and covered the chariots, and the horsemen, and all the host of Pharaoh that came into the sea after them; there remained not so much as one of them.

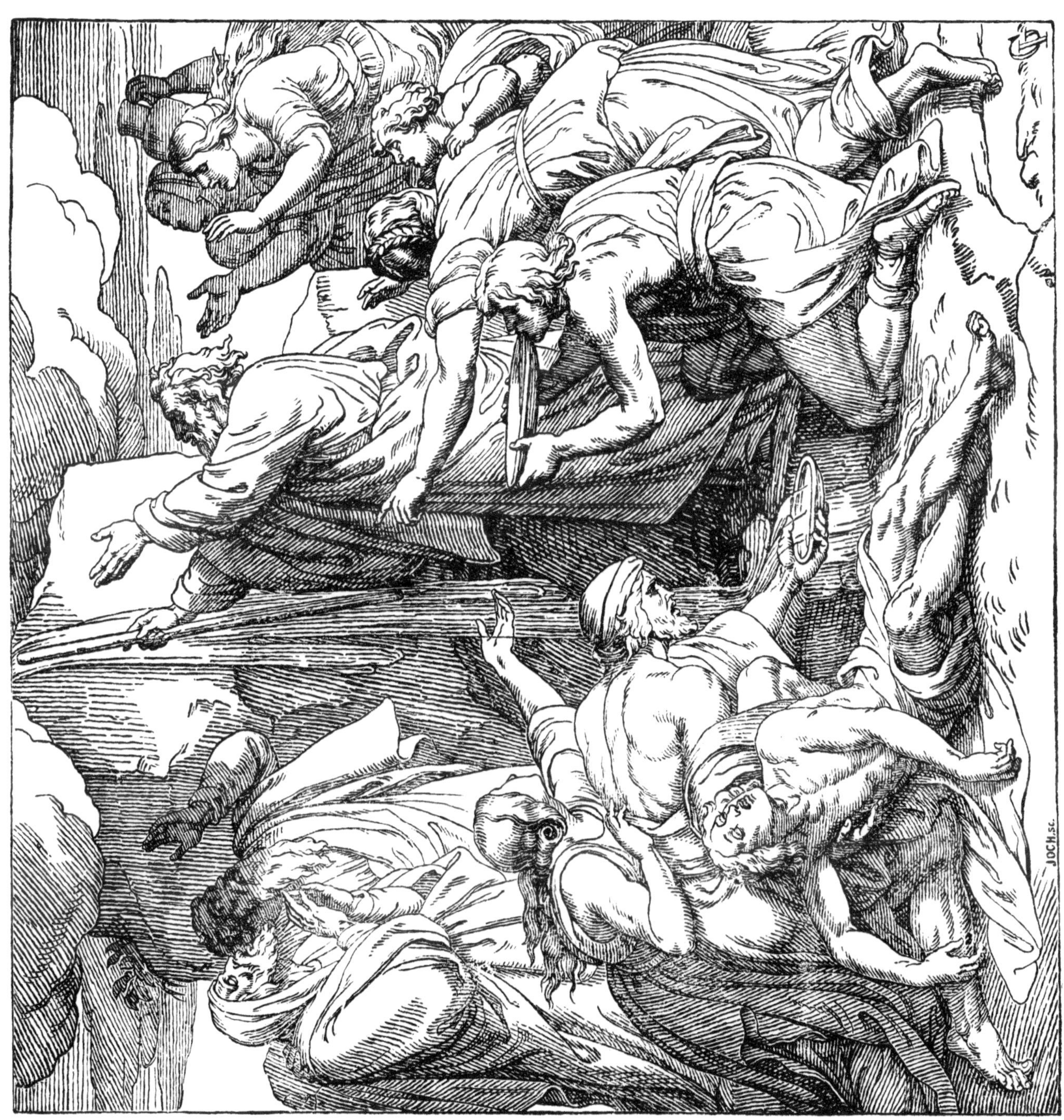

Moses Bringing Water from the Rock

During their exodus from Egypt, Moses and the Israelites came to a place called Rephidim where they wanted water. Instead of being patient, and waiting for God's help, they began to blame Moses. They said, Why have you brought us up out of Egypt to kill us, and our children, and our cattle with thirst?

Then Moses cried to God, and said, What shall I do? The people are almost ready to stone me to death. God said, Go before the people, and take with you the elders of Israel; and take the rod with which you divided the Red Sea. I will go before you, and show you a rock in Horeb which you shall smite with your rod, and out of it shall come water, so that the people may drink. Then Moses went with the elders to the rock in Horeb, and smote it, and waters flowed from it in refreshing streams down to the place where the Israelites had set up their tents. This water lasted them for the whole time that they remained in that neighborhood, which was more than a year.

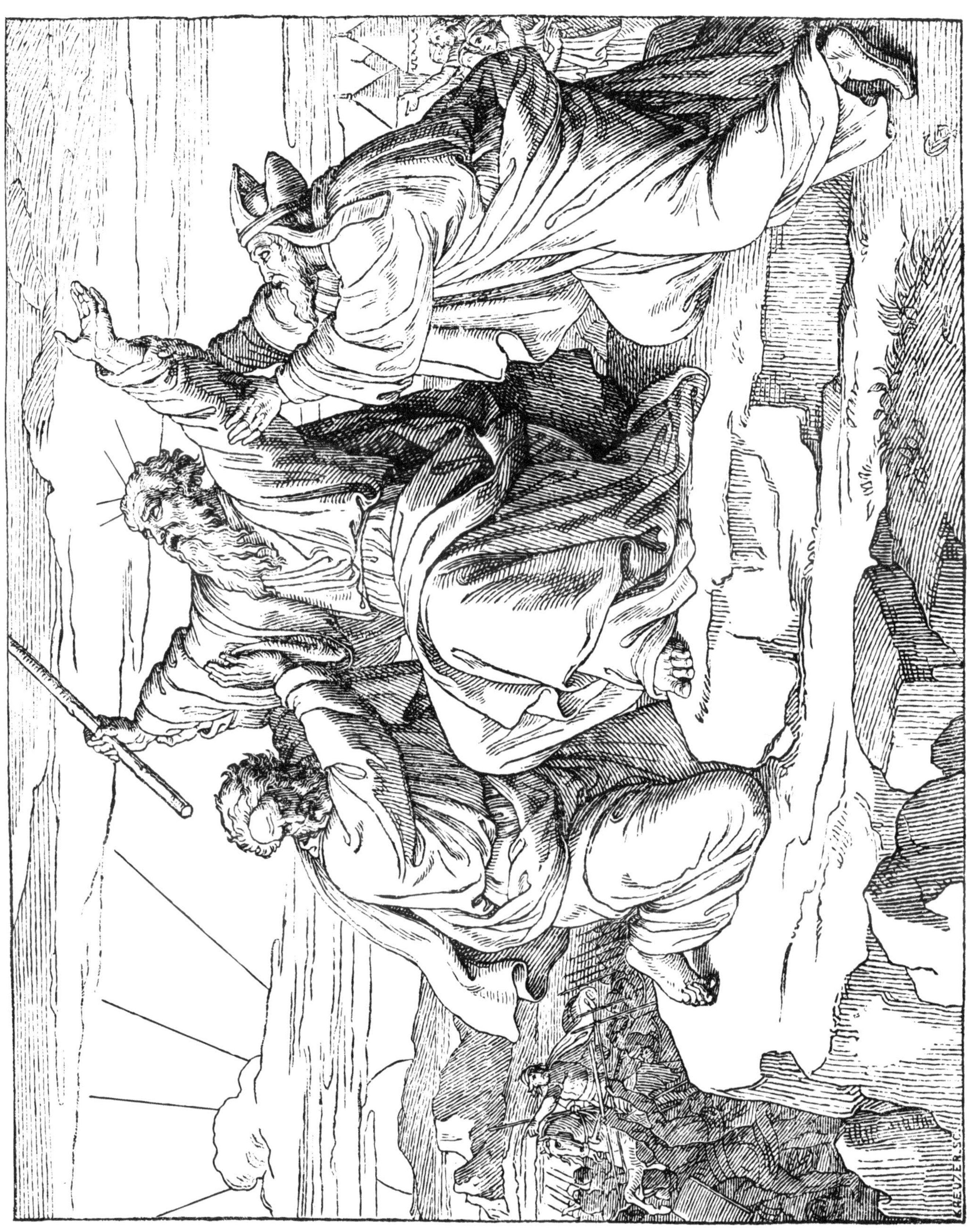

Aaron and Hur Holding Up the Hands of Moses

There came a people called the Amalekites, who fought against the children of Israel in Rephidim. And Moses said to a brave man whose name was Joshua, Choose men, and go out and fight with Amalek; tomorrow I will stand on the top of the hill with the rod of God in my hand. Joshua did as Moses had said. He chose some brave men and went to fight Amalek; and Moses, Aaron and Hur, Miriam's husband, went to the top of the hill where they could see the battle in the valley below.

When Moses held up his hand, the children of Israel were successful and the battle was in their favor, but when Moses let down his hand, Amalek prevailed. Moses was tired, and they brought a stone for him to sit on; his hands were heavy, and so Aaron and Hur held up his hands, one on each side of him. This they did until the sun went down. And Joshua and his men overcame Amalek.

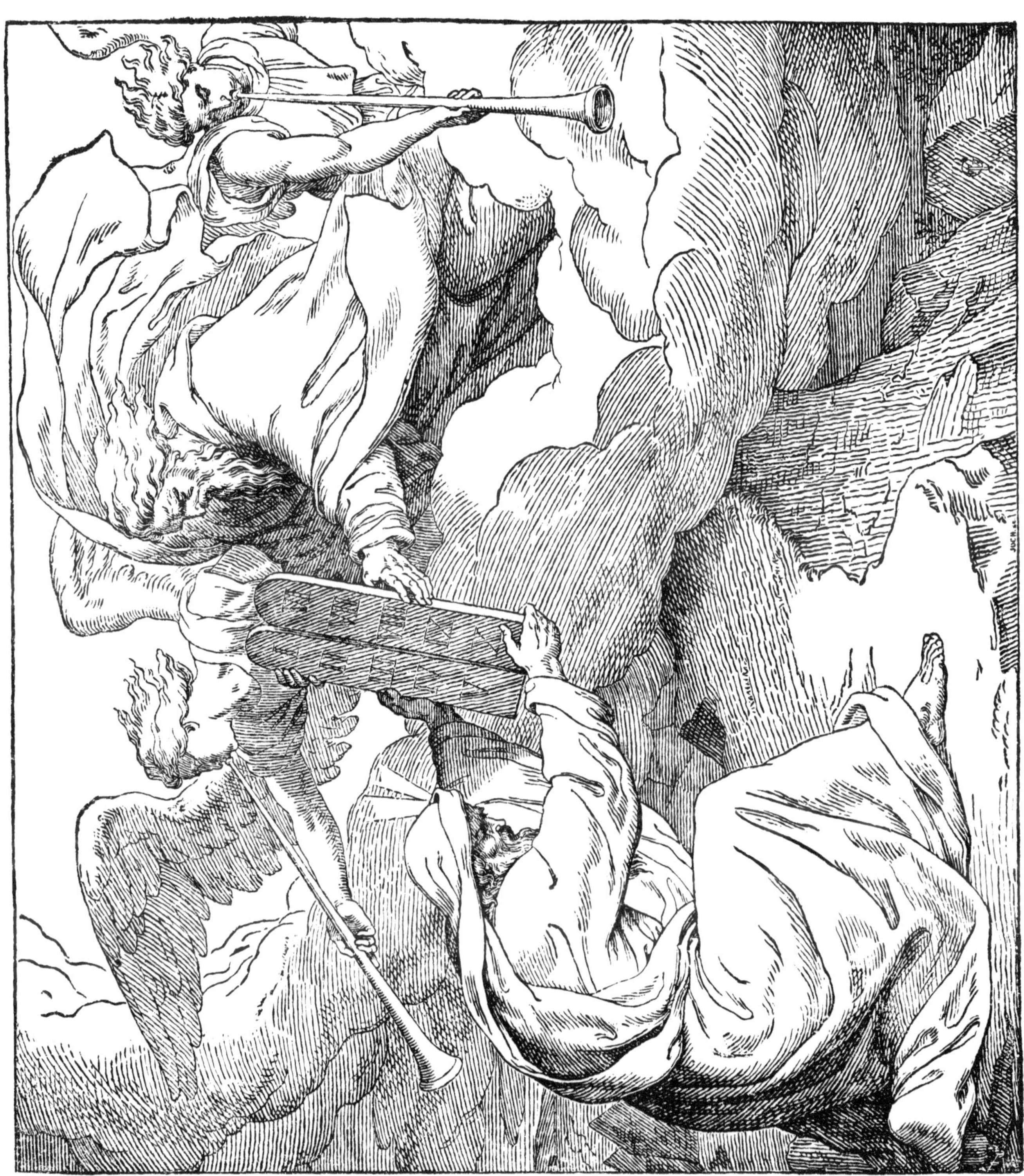

Moses Receiving the Tables of the Law

And Moses chose able men out of all Israel and made them heads over the people, rulers of thousands, rulers of hundreds, rulers of fifties, and rulers of tens. And they judged the people at all seasons: the hard cases they brought unto Moses but every small matter they judged themselves.

The Israelites next came to the desert of Sinai or Horeb, and there they camped before the mountain. This mountain is about three miles in length, and it has two summits or peaks; one is called Mount Horeb, the other Mount Sinai; but Mount Sinai is by far the highest of all the mountains in the whole of that district. This was the place where Moses saw the burning bush, and here they were to wait, while God made known to them his will, and gave to them their laws as a nation. Here it was that God gave the laws which we call " The Ten Commandments."

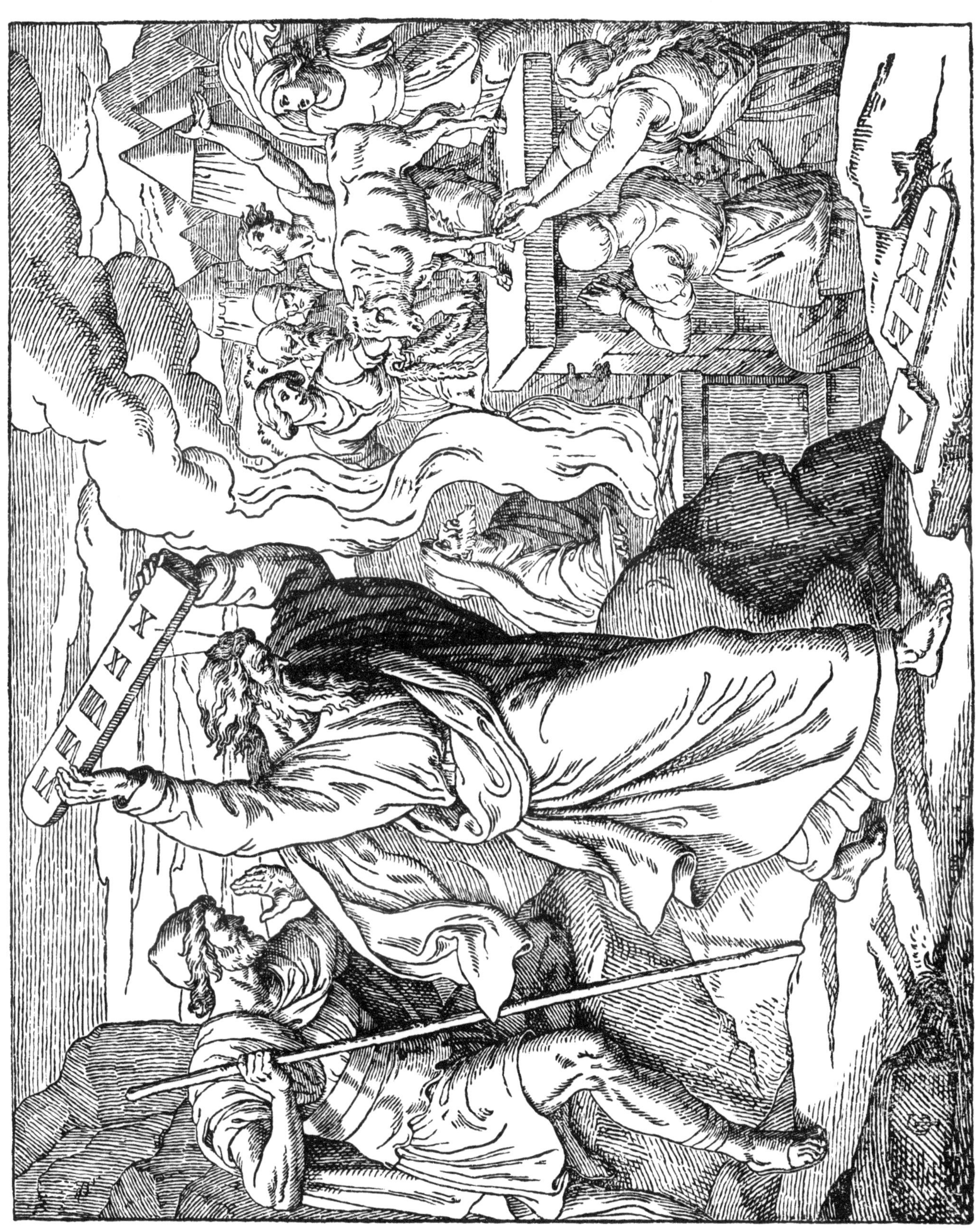

Moses Destroying the Tables of the Law

During the time Moses was up on Mount speaking God, the Israelites were very uneasy because he did not come back. He had been gone for forty days, when the people came to Aaron, and said, Where is Moses? We cannot tell what has become of him: we are afraid he is dead. Make us, therefore an image in the likeness of God, that we may worship before it. Aaron was afraid to tell the people how wicked this was, and he said, Bring me your golden ornaments. And the people were determined to have a likeness of a god, so they took off their ornaments, and brought them to Aaron. Then Aaron made of them the likeness of a calf in gold. Thus they broke the second commandment, where God says, that they were not to make the likeness of anything, to bow down and worship it.

When the image was set up, then all the people came before it, and offered sacrifices and feasted. While they were doing this, God said to Moses, Make haste and go down to the people, for they are sinning. Then Moses went, and he took in his hand the tablets of stone, which were the work of God, and the writing on them was the writing of God, engraven on the tablets. As he came near to the camp, he saw the people dancing round the calf; then he felt very grieved and very angry, and he threw down the tablets, on which God had written his laws and his covenant, and broke them at the bottom of the Mount.

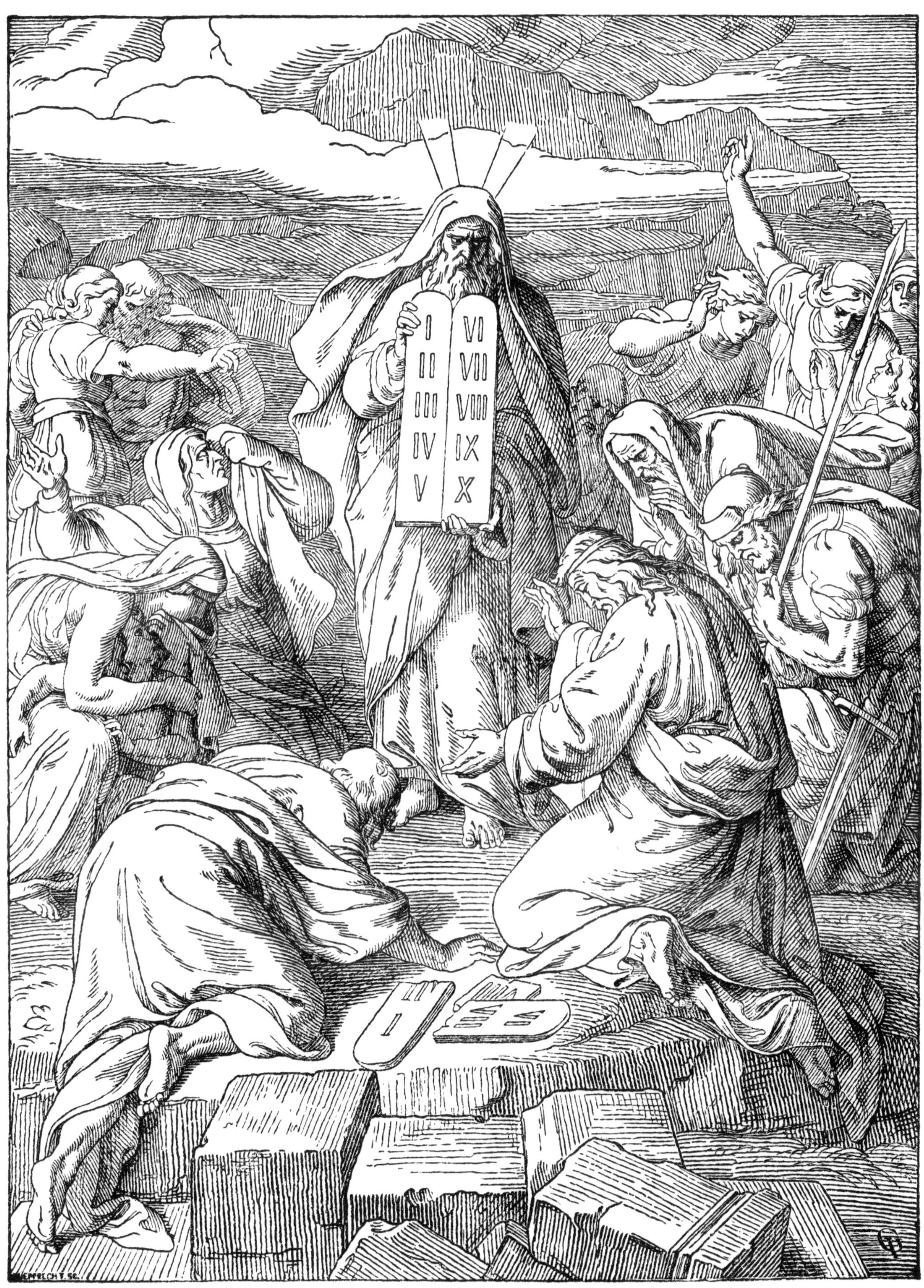
I II III IV V
VI VII VIII IX X

Moses Bringing the New Tables of the Law

Moses took the golden calf that the people had worshipped and burnt it. Then he went back to the mountain, and prayed to God to forgive the people their sin. Afterwards God told Moses to get two more tablets of stone, like those which he had broken. On these God wrote the same laws that he had written on the first tablets.

When Moses came down to the people, they looked at his face, and the skin of his face shone while he talked to the people of all the things that God had shown him, when he was up on Mount Sinai. Moses had been in glorious company, and some of that glory was shared by him.

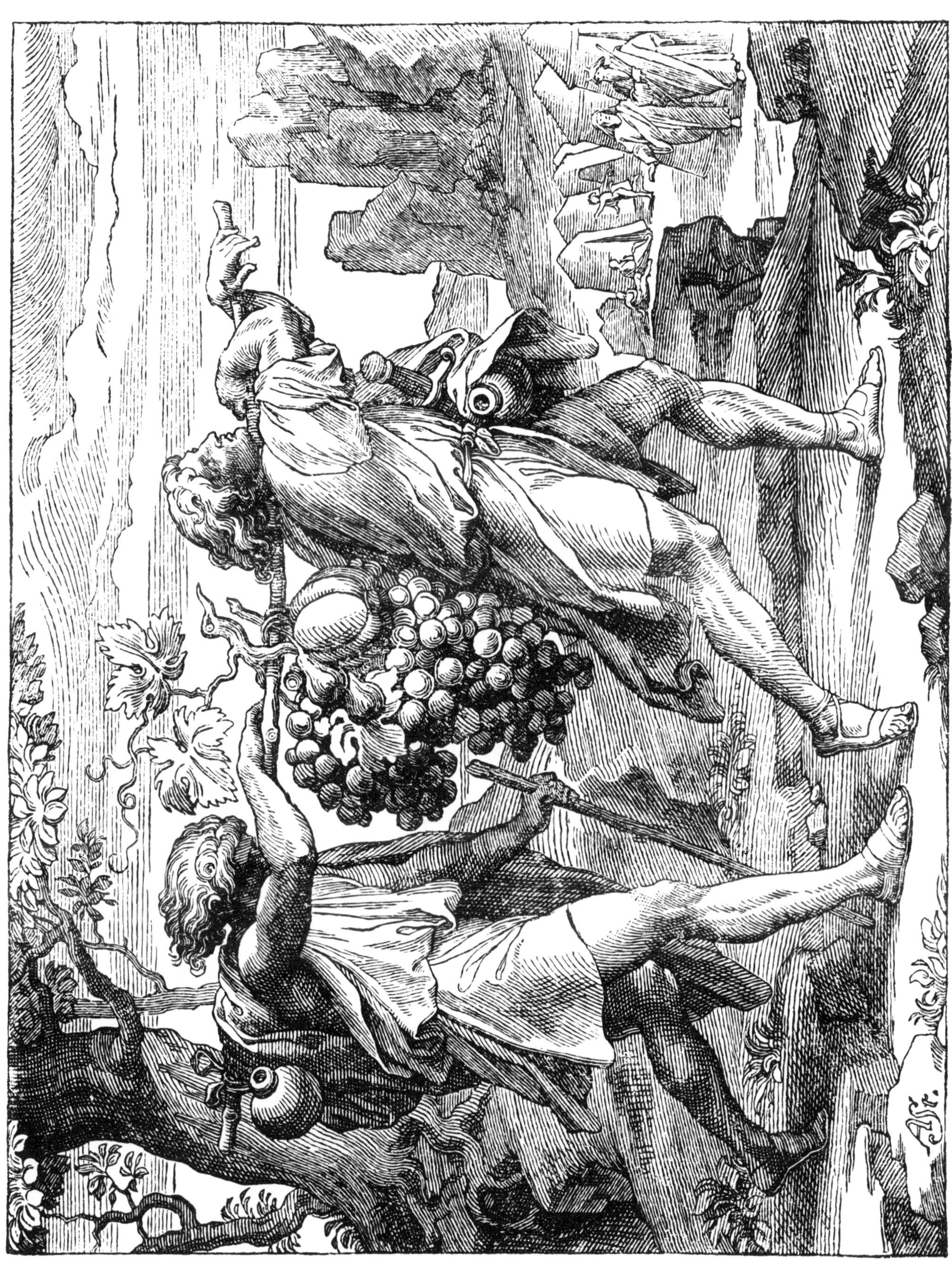

The Spies Returning From Canaan

And God ordered Moses and the Israelites to move toward the Promised Land where they would have a beautiful and settled home. They went on marching and resting, until at last they came to the southern border of the land of Canaan. Now, Moses said, you are in sight of the land which God promised to your fathers: go up and take it; do not be afraid of the people who live in it. But, the people said, We had better send twelve men before us — one man out of each tribe — to search the land, and bring us word again by what me must go up, and into what cities we shall come.

So twelve men were chosen to spy out the land. They left the camp early in September, and came back about the middle of October. They were gone forty days, and they brought back with them some of the fruits which grew in the country to show their countrymen. How delighted they must have been to see the figs, and the grapes, and the pomegranates, which they were told grew in rich abundance in this land which was to be their own! There was one large cluster of grapes, cut from the valley of Eschol, which they looked at with great surprise. It was carried by two men on a pole, partly because of its great size, and partly to keep it from being bruised. The twelve men said, We came unto the land where you sent us, and indeed it floweth with milk, and honey, and this is the fruit of it.

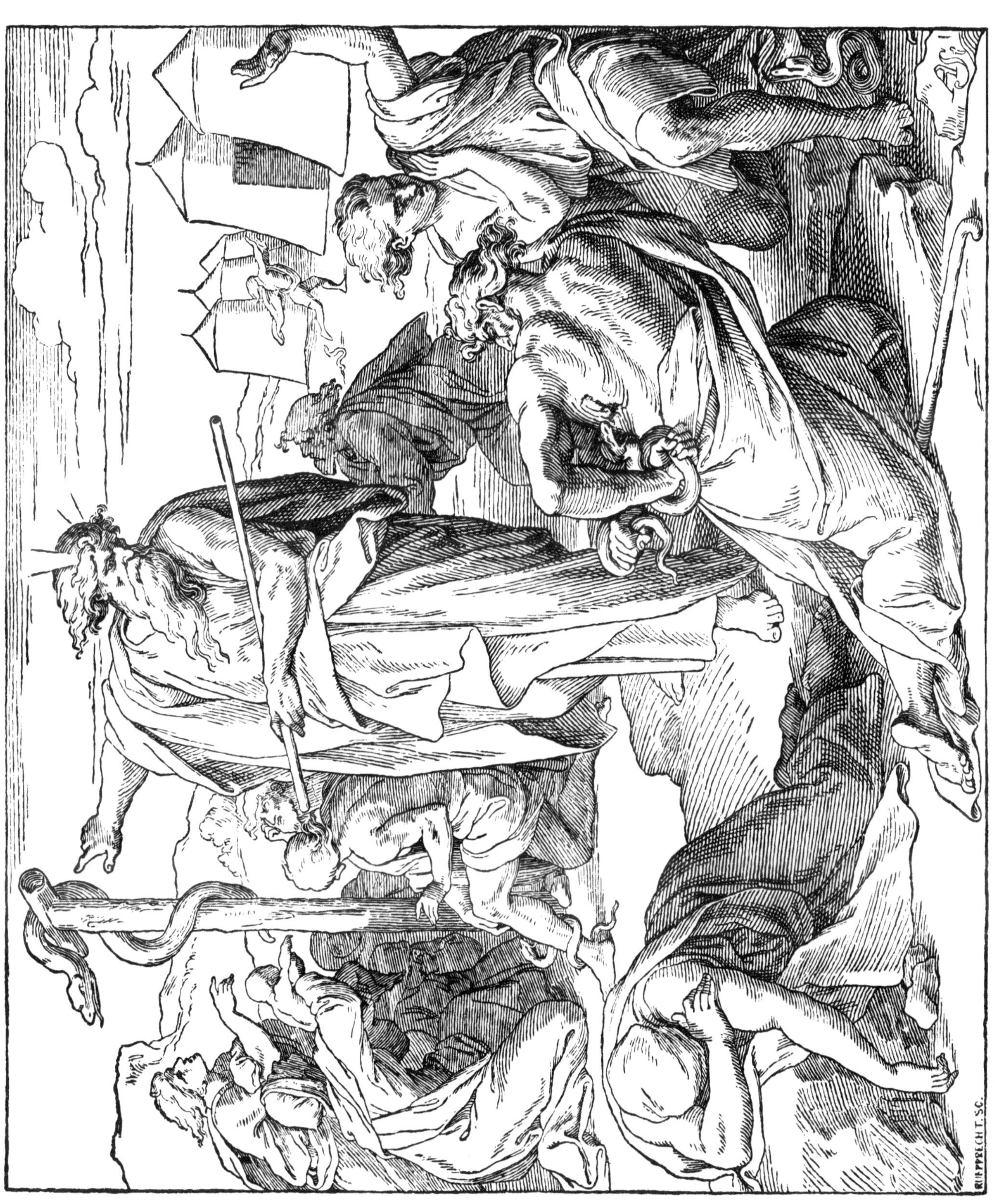

The Brazen Serpent

The Lord said to Moses, Make a serpent of brass, and put it upon a pole, and it shall come to pass that every one that is bitten shall feel well again, when he looks at it. Moses did so; and it came to pass that if a serpent had bitten any man, when he beheld the serpent of brass, he lived.

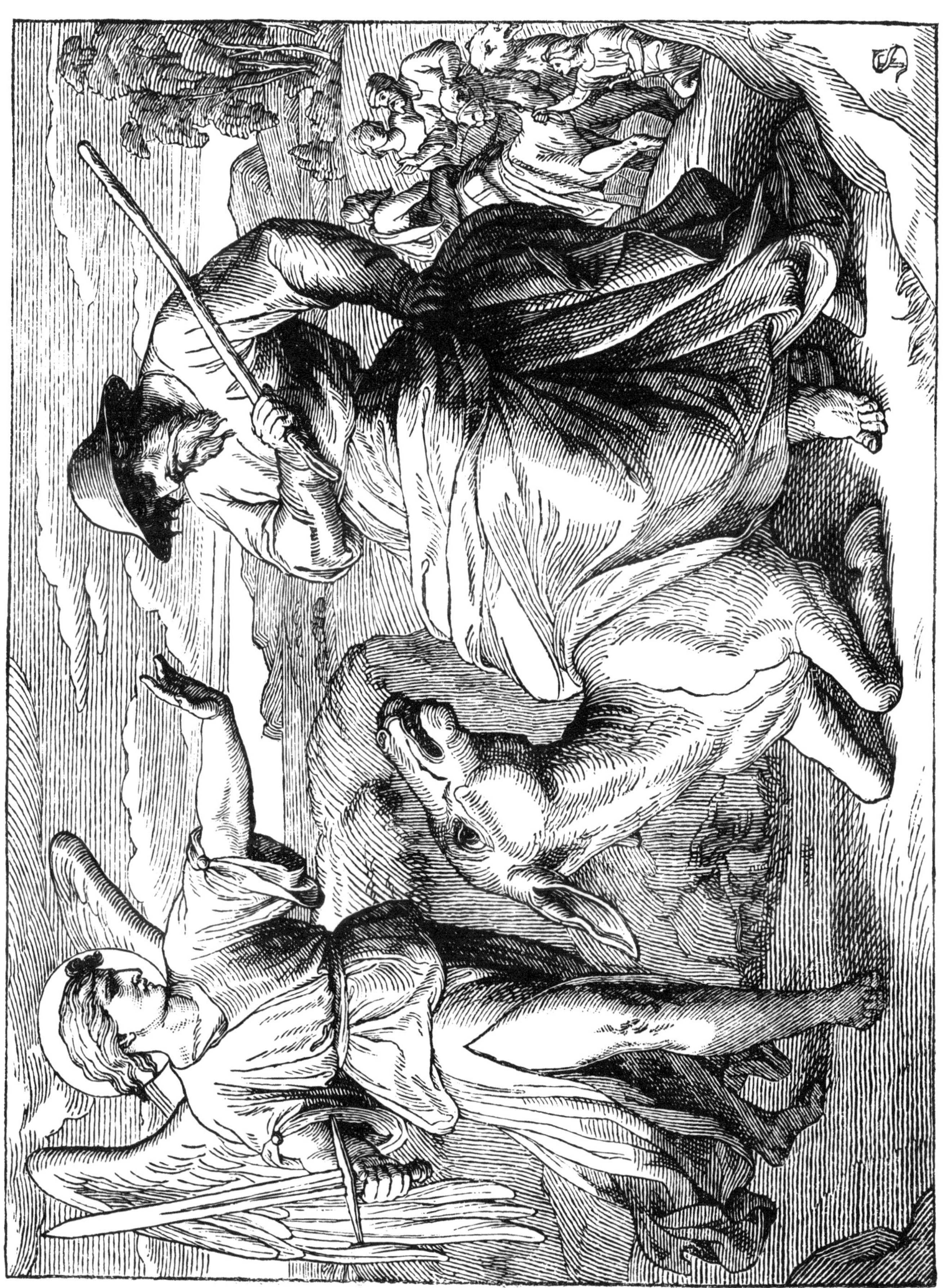

Balaam Met by the Angel of the Lord

As the Israelites sojourned in the plains of Moab, at the close of forty years of wandering, Balak, king of Moab, feared that the Israelites were about to destroy his people, just as they had destroyed the Amorites. And Balak sent princes to the prophet Balaam to induce him to come and curse the Israelites. But Balaam sent word that God had told him in a dream not to go. Then Balak sent again princes, more honorable and with richer gifts; and God said to Balaam: Go with them; yet the word which I shall say to thee, that shalt thou do.

And Balaam rose up in the morning, and saddled his donkey and went with the princes of Moab. And God's anger was kindled because Balaam loved the wages of unrighteousness, and the angel of the Lord stood in the way for an adversary against him. And the donkey saw the Angel of the Lord standing in the way, and his sword drawn in his hand; and the donkey turned aside out of the way, and went into the field; and Balaam smote the donkey to turn her into the way.

But the Angel of the Lord stood in a path, shut in by vineyard walls on each side. And when the donkey saw the Angel of the Lord, she thrust herself unto the wall and crushed Balaam's foot against the wall; and he smote her again. And the Angel of the Lord went further and stood in a narrow place, where was no way to turn either to the right hand or to the left. And when the donkey saw the Angel, she fell down under Balaam; and Balaam's anger was kindled, and he smote the donkey with a staff.

And the Lord opened the mouth of the donkey, and she said to Balaam: What have I done unto thee, that thou has smitten me these three times? And Balaam said to the donkey, because thou has mocked me; I wish there were a sword in my hand, for then I would kill thee. Then the Lord opened the eyes of Balaam, and he saw the Angel of the Lord standing in the way, and his sword in his hand; and Balaam bowed himself and fell to the ground, and said to the Angel of the Lord, I have sinned; now therefore, if it displease thee, I will return. And the Angel of the Lord said to Balaam, Go with the men, but only the word that I shall speak unto thee, shalt thou speak.

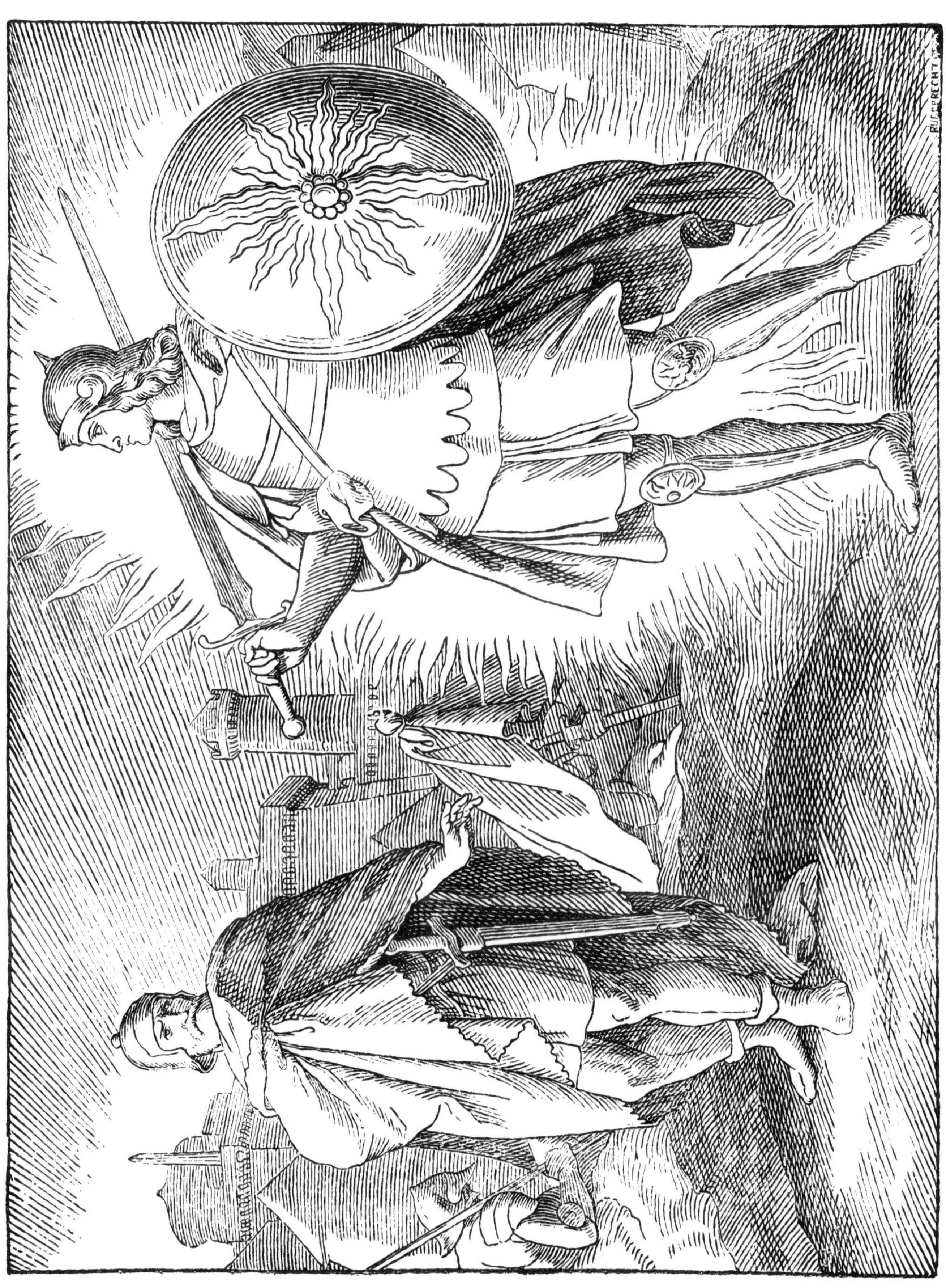

The Angel Appearing to Joshua

Before Moses died, he chose Joshua to be the leader of the people after him, for so the Lord commanded him. And Joshua would lead the children of Israel into the Promised Land which the Lord sware unto them, and the Lord would be with him.

And Joshua went up to see the city of Jericho, and to devise how it might be taken. And as he looked he had a vision of a man standing over him with a drawn sword in his hand. Then Joshua went unto him, and said, Art thou for us or against us? And the man answered, Nay, but as captain of the Lord's host am I come. Then Joshua fell on his face to the earth, and did worship, and said, What saith my Lord unto his servant? And the captain of the Lord's host said unto Joshua, Loose thy shoe from off thy foot, for the place whereon thou standest is holy. And Joshua did so. Then the angel told Joshua how he should take the city of Jericho.

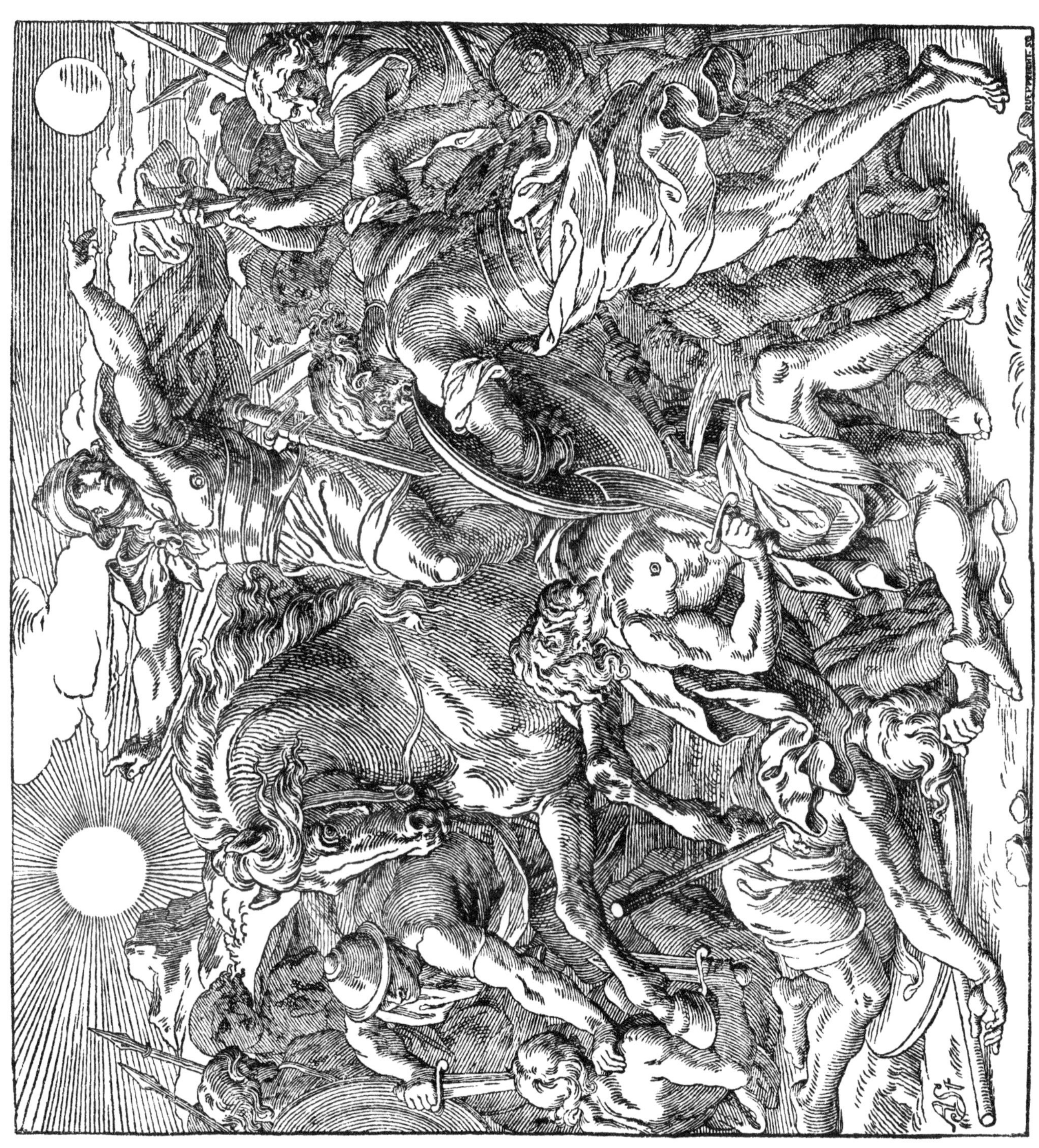

JOSHUA COMMANDING THE SUN TO STAND STILL

When Joshua saw the Amorites fleeing down the pass, he feared lest the sun should go down before Israel had made an end of destroying their enemy. Therefore he cried aloud, Sun, stand thou still upon Gibeon; and thou, moon, in the valley of Ajalon. And it was so that the light failed not the children of Israel till they had avenged themselves on their enemies.

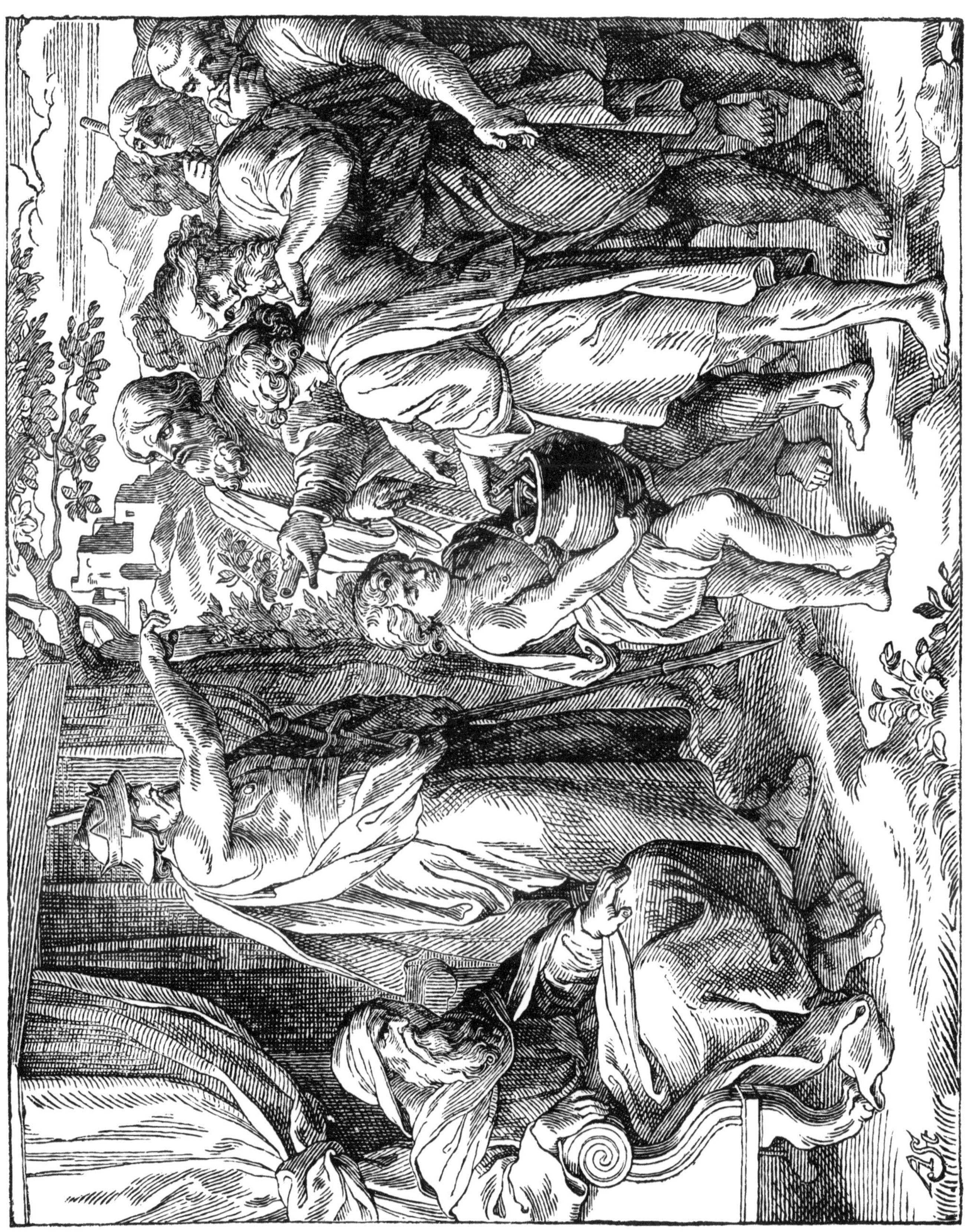

Joshua Dividing the Land

Joshua divided the land of Canaan among the tribes; and while he did so, Caleb came to him, and said, Thou knowest the thing that the Lord said unto Moses the man of God concerning me and thee in Kadesh-barnea. Forty years old was I when Moses sent me from Kadesh-barnea to spy out the land; and I brought him word again as it was in mine heart. Nevertheless my brethren that went with me made the heart of the people melt for fear of their report; but I wholly followed the Lord my God.

And Moses sware on that day, saying, Surely the land whereon thy feet have trodden shall be thine inheritance, and thy children's for ever, because thou hast wholly followed the Lord my God. And now the Lord hath kept me alive, as he said, these forty-and-five years, even since the Lord spake this word unto Moses, while the children of Israel wandered in the wilderness. And yet I am as strong this day as I was in the day that Moses sent me. Now therefore give me this mountain, whereof the Lord spake in that day; for my brethren that went with me to espy the land spake of the children of Anak that were there, and of the strong cities in which they dwelt, and made the heart of the people to melt with their report. But if the Lord be with me, I shall be able to drive them out as the Lord said. Then Joshua blessed Caleb, and gave him Hebron for an inheritance.

When the land had been divided, Joshua further appointed six cities, three on either side of Jordan, to which any man might flee who should kill another unwittingly. Also to the tribe of Levi forty-eight cities were given out of the portions of the tribes.

So Joshua rested from his labors, dwelling in Timnath-serah in Mount Ephraim, for this had been given to him for his inheritance; and among all the portions of the children of Israel there was none humbler than his. And when fifteen years had passed, and he knew that his end was drawing nigh, he sent for the elders of Israel to his house at Timnath, and said to them, I am old and stricken in age. And ye have seen what the Lord hath done for you, how he has driven out the nations of the land before you, and divided the land unto you for an inheritance. Keep, therefore, all that is written in the book of the law of Moses; turn not aside from it to the right hand or to the left.

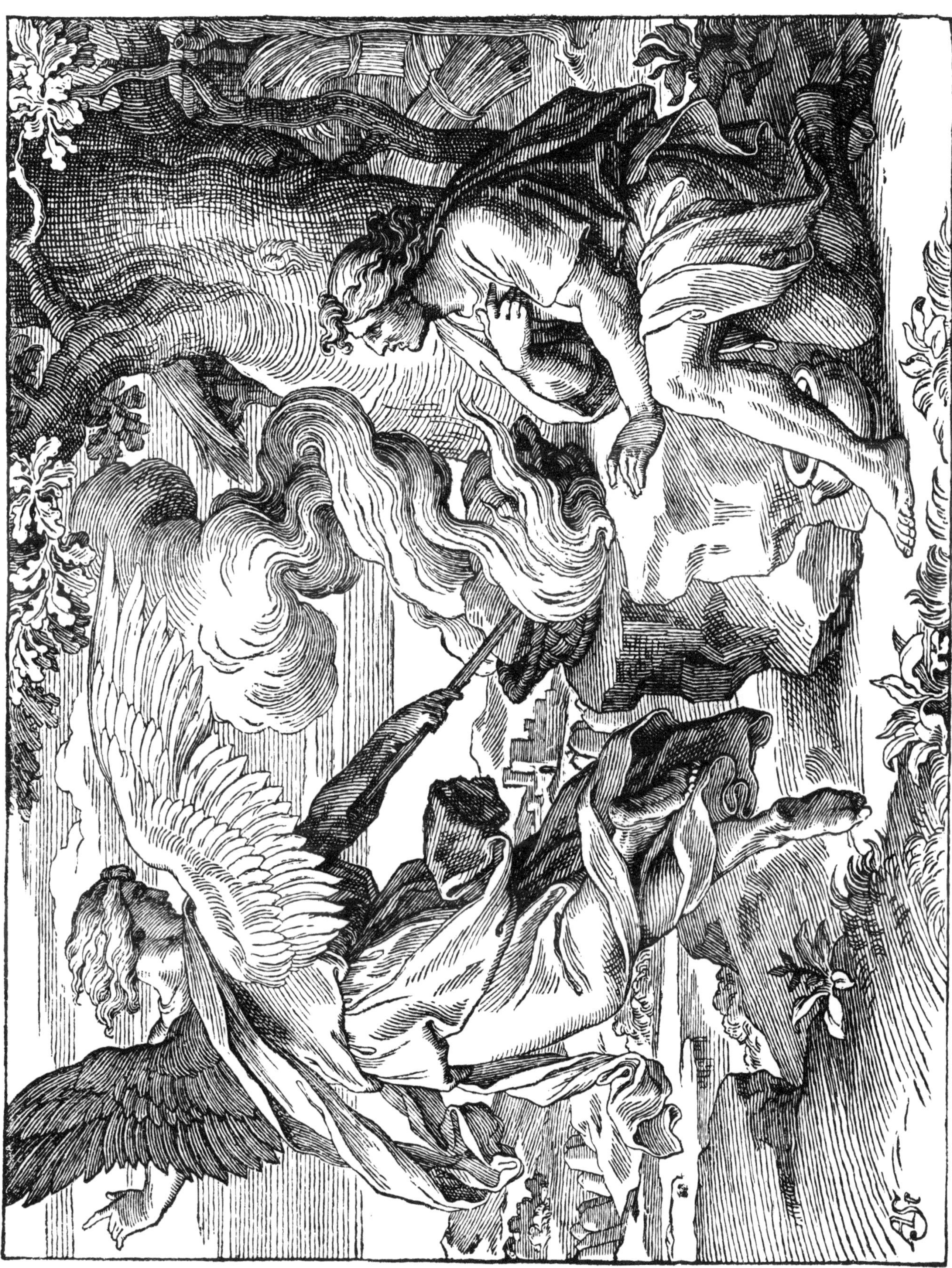

Gideon's Offering Burnt by Fire from the Rock

Now there dwelt in Ophrah of Manasseh a certain Joash, of the house of Abiezer. The Midianites had slain his sons, having taken them at Mount Tabor, where they had gone to meet the princes of Israel at the sanctuary that was on the top of the mount. Only Gideon was left to him. This Gideon was threshing wheat with a flail in the wine-press, doing it secretly for fear of the Midianites.

There came an angel of the Lord and sat under the oak that was in Ophrah, and appeared unto him, and said, The Lord is with thee, thou mighty man of valor. Gideon said, If the Lord be with me, why then is all this befallen us? And where are all his miracles that our fathers told us of, saying, Did not the Lord bring you up out of Egypt? But now the Lord hath forsaken us, and delivered us into the hand of the Midianites.

The Lord said unto him by his angel, Go in this thy might, and thou shalt save Israel from the hand of the Midianites. And Gideon said, Wherewith shall I save Israel? My family is the weakest in Manasseh, and I am the youngest in my father's house.

The Lord said unto him, Surely I will be with thee, and thou shalt smite the Midianites as though they were but one man. And Gideon said unto the Lord, If I have found grace in thy sight, then show me a sign that thou dost in truth talk with me. Depart not hence, I pray thee, until I come unto thee, and bring my meat-offering, and set it before thee. Then Gideon went in and made ready a kid of the goats, and made unleavened cakes of flour: the flesh he put in a basket and the broth in a pot, and he brought out the offering unto the angel as he sat under the oak, and presented them.

The Angel of Jehovah said unto him, Take the flesh and the unleavened cakes, and lay them upon the rock, and pour out the broth over the offering upon the rock. And Gideon did so.

Then the Angel of the Lord put out the staff that was in his hand, for he had the semblance of a traveller, and touched the flesh and unleavened cakes, and there rose up fire out of the rock, and consumed the flesh and the unleavened cakes. Then the Angel of the Lord departed out of his sight And when Gideon perceived that he was indeed an Angel of the Lord, he said, O Lord God! I have seen an Angel of the Lord face to face. And the Lord said unto him, Peace be unto thee; fear not: thou shalt not die.

And it came to pass that same night that the Lord said unto him, Take thy father's young bullock, and the seven year old bullock also, and throw down the altar of Baal that thy father hath, and break down the idol that is by it. And put the stones of the altar and the wood of the idol on the bullocks, and carry them to the top of the rock. There shalt thou build with the stones an altar to the Lord thy God, and lay the wood of the idol in order upon the altar, and slay the second bullock, and offer it for a burnt-offering with the wood of the idol.

So Gideon took ten men of his servants, and did as the Lord had said unto him; but because he feared the house of his father, and the men of the city, for these were Amorites, he did it by night. And when the men of the city rose up early in the morning, the altar of Baal was cast down, and the idol that stood by it was cut down, and there was another altar built, and on this the seven year old bullock had been offered.

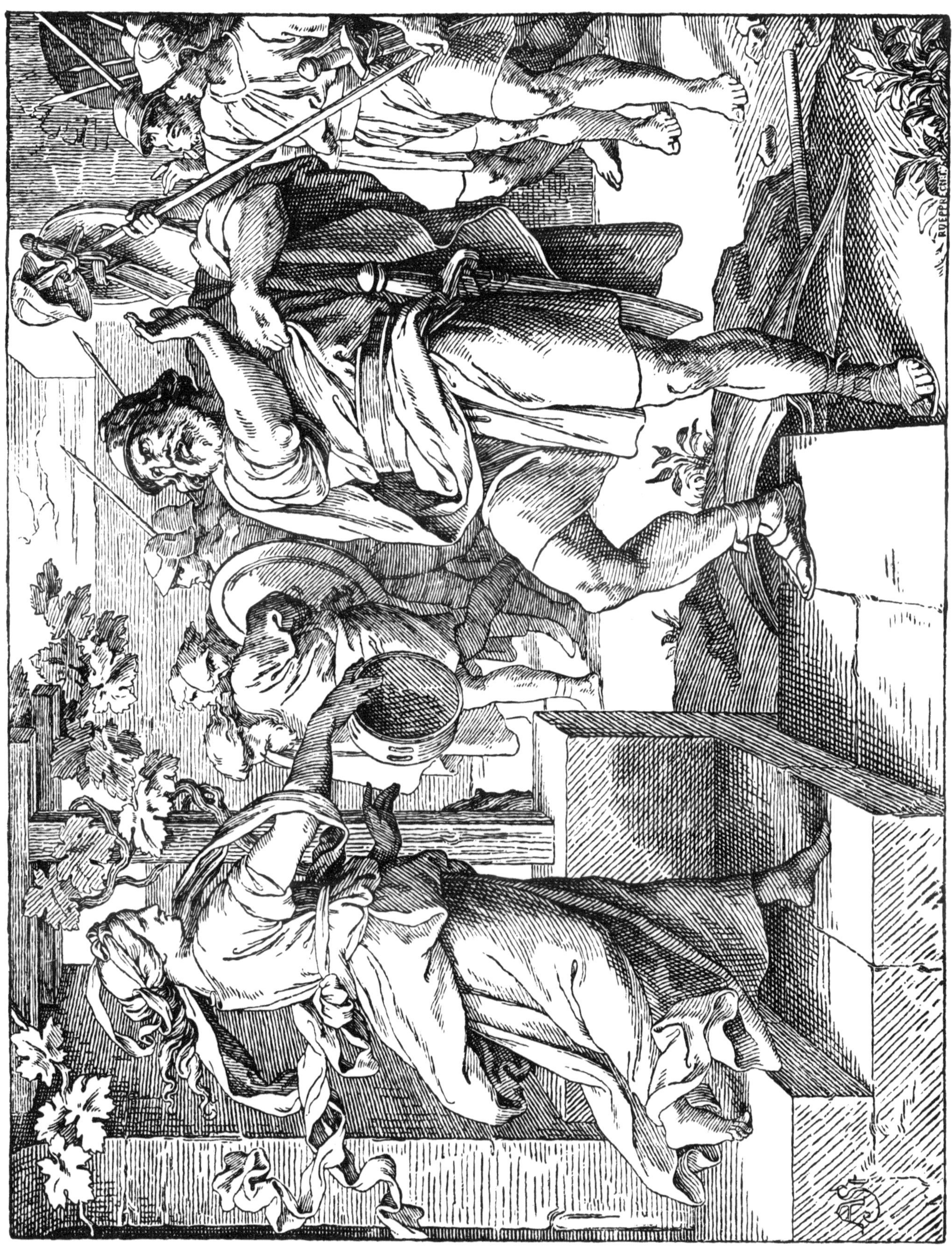

Jephthah Meeting his Daughter

As soon as Gideon was dead, the children of Israel returned to their wicked ways. In the course of time, the Ammonites made war against Israel. And the children of Israel sent for a man named Jephthah, a skillful warrior, to be their captain, and lead them forth to battle. Jephthah said he would go with them if they would promise to make him a prince and a ruler in the land. This they said they would do, and Jephthah took his place as captain at the head of the army of Israel. But before he left his home in Mizpeh, Jephthah vowed a vow to the Lord, and said, If thou wilt deliver the children of Ammon into my hands, I will offer up as a burnt offering whatever comes out of my house to meet me, when I return to my home in peace.

Jephthah fought against the Ammonites and overthrew them, and afterwards departed for his home in Mizpeh. As he drew near his house, the one that came forth to meet him was his own daughter, his only child, in whom his heart was bound up. She, with her fair companions, came to meet the returning hero, with timbrels in hand and with songs and dances.

As soon as Jephthah saw her, he rent his robes, and cried out, Alas my daughter! thou hast brought me very low, for I have given my word to the Lord, and cannot take it back. Nor did she ask it. She replied that he must do to her according as he had promised the Lord, who had given him the victory. Only, she said, let me alone for two months, that I may go up and down the mountains, I and my companions, and lament my fate.

Jephthah granted her request, and at the end of two months she came back to her father, and he sacrificed her according to the vow he had made. And it became a custom for the daughters of Israel to mourn over the daughter of Jephthah for four days in every year.

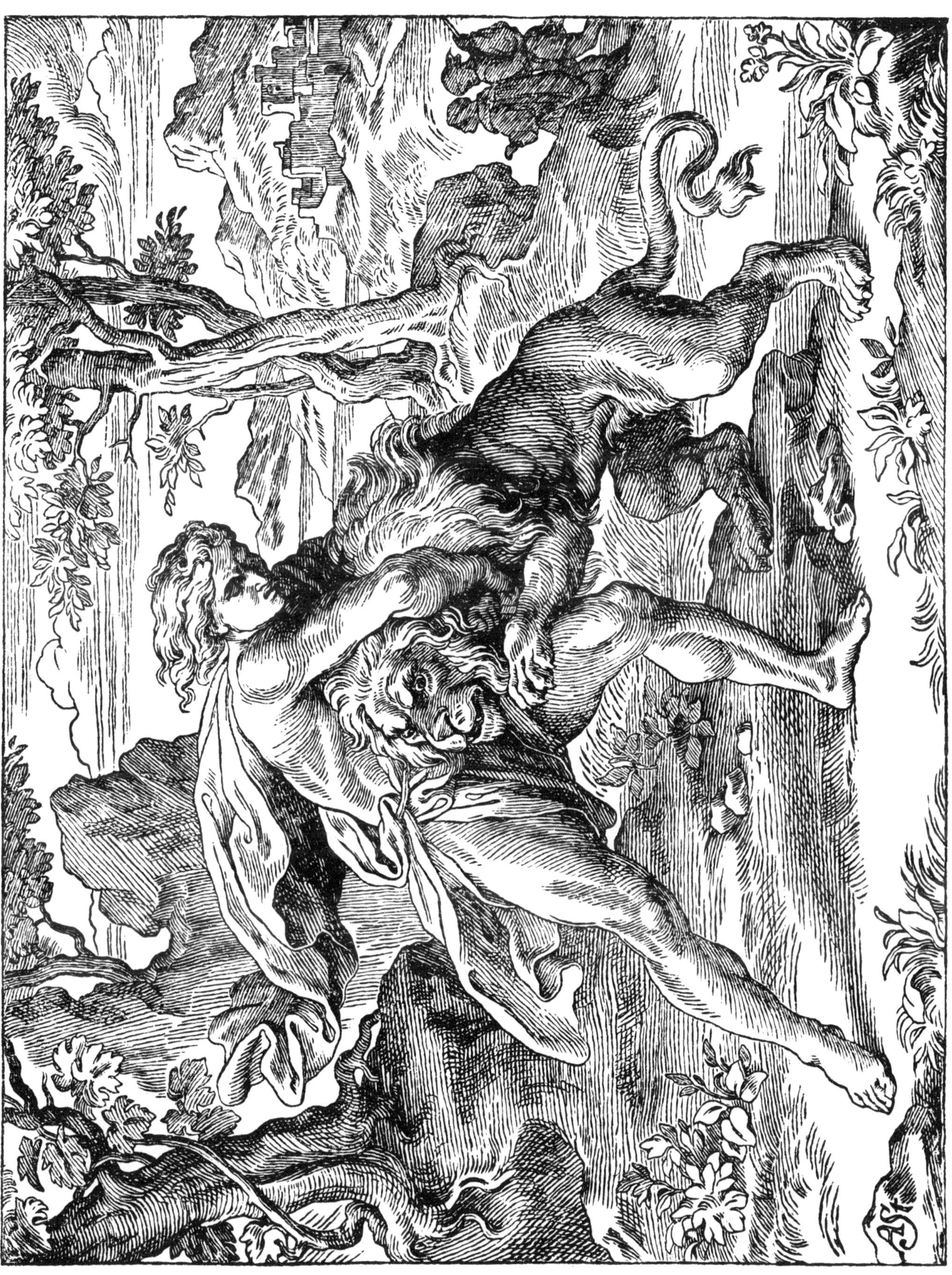

Samson Slaying the Lion

Now there was on the plain below Zorah a certain village named Timnath. It was a village of the inheritance of Dan; but the Philistines dwelt there at this time. Samson went down thither, and saw a woman of the daughters of the Philistines that pleased him. Then he came up to Zorah, and said to his father and his mother, I have seen a woman in Timnath of the daughters of the Philistine; now, therefore, get her for me to wife.

Then his father and his mother him, Is there never a woman among all the daughters of thy brethren that are of the same tribe with thee, nor yet of the other tribes of Israel, that thou goest to take a wife of the uncircumcised Philistines?

Then Samson said to his father, Get her for me; for she pleaseth me well. But his father and his mother knew not that this was of the Lord, that their son might find occasion against the Philistines; for at that time the Philistines had dominion over Israel.

Then went Samson down, and his father and his mother, to Timnath. But Samson parted from his company, going by the way of the vineyards. And as he went, a young lion roared against him. And the Spirit of the Lord came mightily upon him, and he rent the lion as he would have rent a kid, and this with no weapon in his hand. But he told not his father and his mother what he had done. After this he went down and talked with the woman, and she pleased him well.

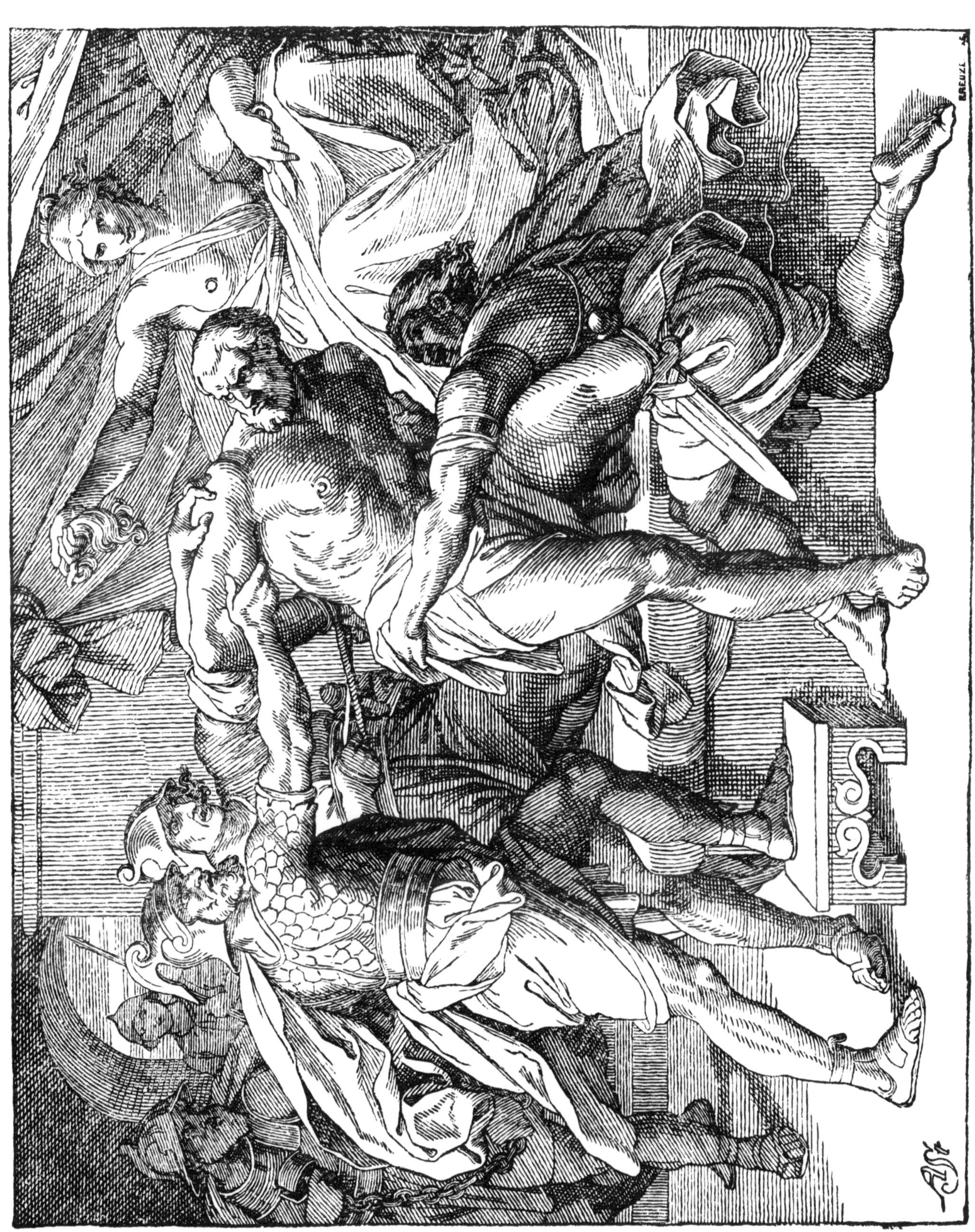

Samson Caught and Bound by his Foes

Samson loved a woman whose name was Delilah. And the lords of the cities of the Philistines came to her and said unto her, Entice him, and see wherein his great strength lieth, and by what means we may prevail against him, that we may bind him to afflict him; and we will give thee, every one of us, eleven hundred pieces of silver. So Delilah said to Samson, Tell me, I pray thee, wherein thy great strength lieth, and how thou mightest be bound. Samson said, If they bind me with seven green twigs of the willow tree, then shall I be weak, and be as another man.

Then the lords of the Philistines brought to her seven green twigs, and she bound him with them. Now there were men lying in wait, in the very chamber with her; so when she bound him, she said, The Philistines be upon thee, Samson! And he brake the twigs as easily as if they were charred in a fire. So the secret of his strength was not known.

After awhile Delilah said to Samson, Thou hast mocked me, and told me lies: now tell me wherewith thou mightest in truth be bound. And he said unto her, If they bind me with new ropes, then shall I be weak, and be as another man. Delilah, therefore, took new ropes and bound him therewith, and said unto him, The Philistines be upon thee, Samson! And there were, as before, men that laid wait in the chamber. Then Samson brake the new ropes off his arms as if they had been a thread.

Yet again Delilah said to Samson, Hitherto thou hast mocked me, and told me lies; tell me wherewith thou mightest be bound. He said unto her, Thou canst do it if thou weavest the seven locks of my hair into the web of thy loom, and fastenest them with the pin to the wall. For his hair was long and hung down in seven locks. So Delilah wove the locks, and fastened them with the pin to the wall. Then she said unto him, The Philistines be upon thee, Samson! And he awaked out of his sleep, and went away with the web into which his hair was woven, and the pin, and the beam itself.

Once again she said to him, How canst thou say I love thee, when thy heart is not with me? Thou hast mocked me these three times, and hast not told me wherein thy great strength lieth. And when she pressed him daily with her words, and urged him so that his soul was vexed unto death, he told her all his heart, and said, There hath not come a razor on my head; for I have been a Nazarite unto God: if I be shaven, then will my strength go from me, and I shall become weak like any other man. And when Delilah saw that he had told her all his heart, she sent and called the lords of the Philistines, saying, Come up again yet this once, for he hath showed me all his heart.

Then the lords of the Philistines came and brought their money in their hand. And Delilah made Samson sleep with his head on her knees, and as he slept she caused a man to cut off the seven locks of his hair. So she robbed him of his strength. Then she said, The Philistines be upon thee, Samson! And he awoke and said, I will go as before and shake myself. For he knew not that the Lord had departed from him. But the Philistines took him, and put out his eyes, and brought him down to Gaza, and bound him with fetters of brass, and made him grind the mill in the prison house.

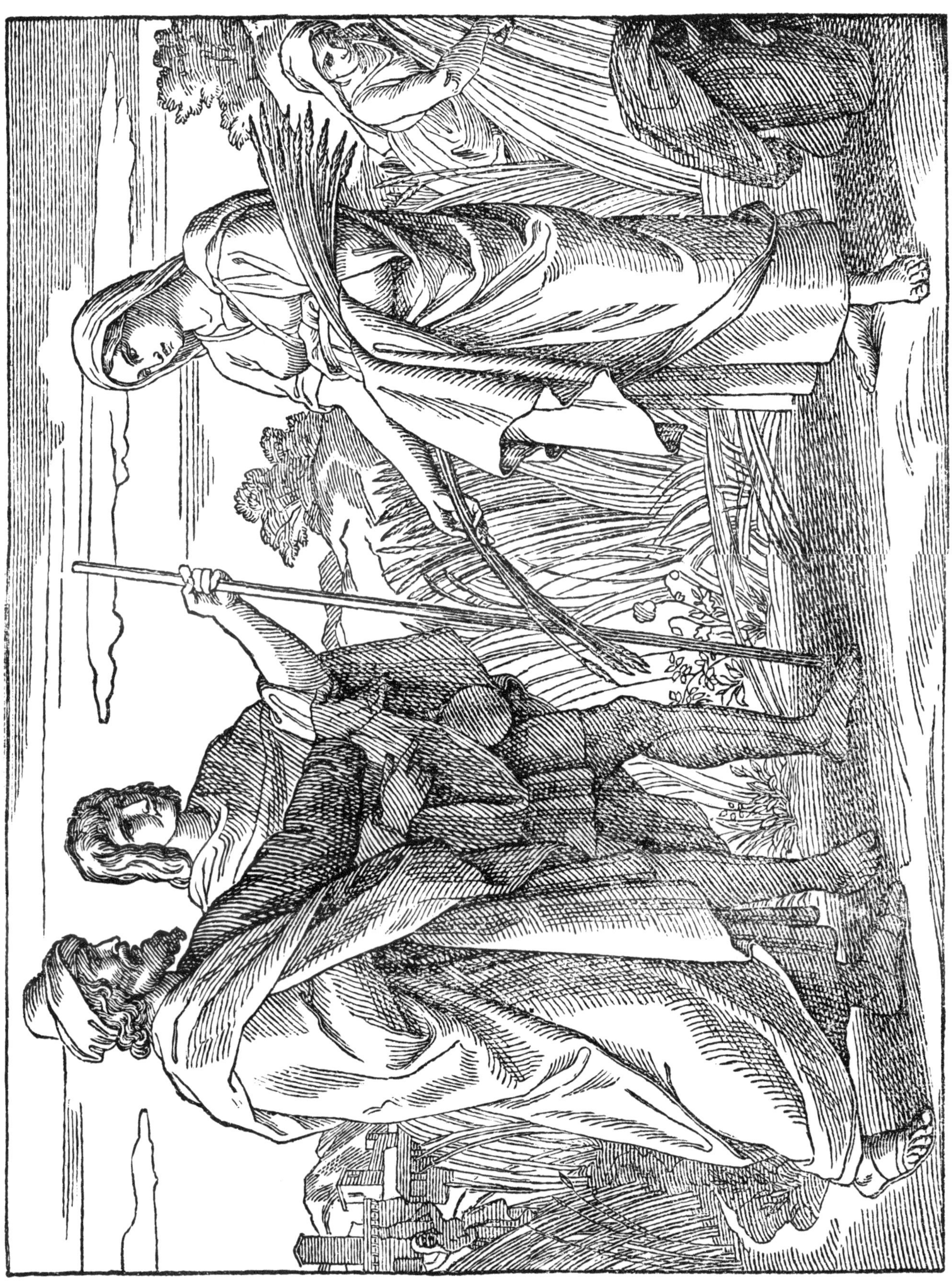

Ruth Gleaning in the Fields of Boaz

Now the time when Naomi and Ruth came to Bethlehem was at the beginning of barley harvest. There was in Bethlehem a certain man that was a kinsman of Elimelech, the husband of Naomi who had died. His name was Boaz, and he was very rich. Ruth said to her mother-in-law, Let me now go to the field and glean ears of corn after anyone in whose sight I may find favor. And Naomi said to her, Go, my daughter. So she went and gleaned in the field, after the reapers; and she gathered in a portion of the field which belonged to Boaz. And behold Boaz came from Bethlehem, and said to his reapers, The Lord be with you! and they answered him, The Lord bless thee!

Then Boaz said to the servant that was over the reapers, Whose damsel is this? The man said, This is the damsel that came back with Naomi out of the land of Moab. She said to me, Let me glean after the reapers. So she came, and hath continued from the morning until now, and hath scarcely rested at all. Then Boaz said to her, Go not to glean in another field; abide here, keeping close to my maidens. None shall harm thee. And when thou art thirsty, go to the vessels, and drink of that which the men have drawn.

When she heard this, she fell on her face before him on the ground, and said, Why dost thou take notice of me, seeing that I am but a stranger? Boaz answered, I have heard all that thou hast done to thy mother-in-law, and how that thou hast left thy father and thy mother, and hast come to a people which before thou knewest not. The Lord, under whose wings thou art come to seek refuge, recompense thee for it!

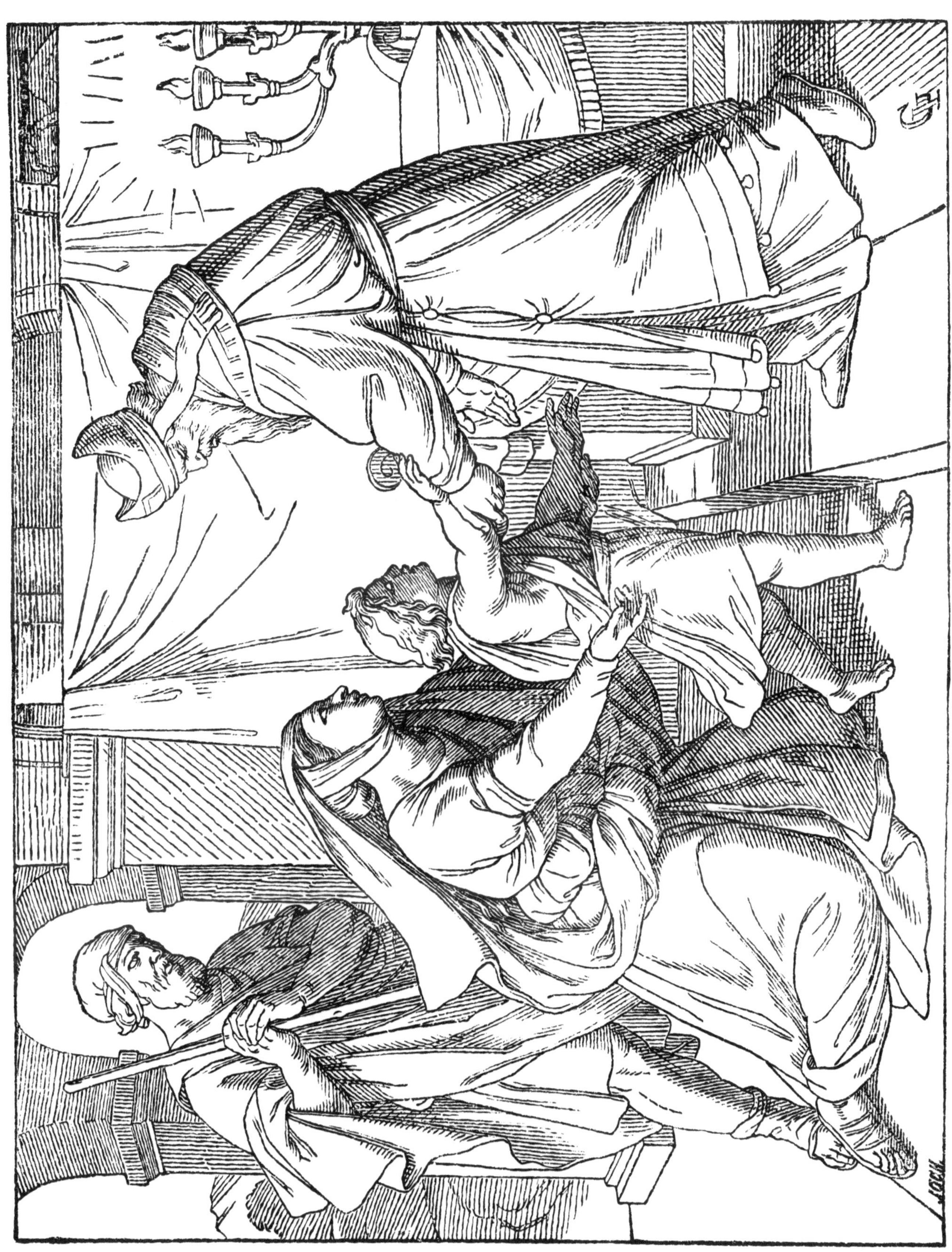

THE YOUNG SAMUEL BROUGHT TO ELI

In Ramah, which is in the hill-country of Ephraim, there dwelt a man of the tribe of Levi, Elkanah by name. He had two wives; the name of the one was Hannah, and the name of the other Peninnah; and Peninnah had children, but Hannah had none.

Now, in a certain year when they had sacrificed and had sat down to eat and drink, Hannah rose up quickly from the table, and went to the tabernacle. And Eli the high priest sat upon his throne, by the door of the inner court of the tabernacle. And Hannah had great bitterness of soul, and prayed unto the Lord, and wept sore, And she vowed a vow and said, O Lord of Hosts, if thou wilt indeed look on the affliction of thine handmaid, and remember me, and not forget thine handmaid, but wilt give unto thine handmaid a man child, then will I give him unto the Lord all the days of his life, and there shall no razor come upon his head.

Then Eli answered and said, Go in peace: and the God of Israel grant thee thy petition that thou hast asked of him. And Hannah said, Let thine handmaid find grace in thy sight. And she went her way, and returned to her husband, where he sat at meat with Peninnah and his children, and did eat, and was no more sorrowful. In due time Hannah bare a son, and she called his name Samuel, for she said, I have asked him of the Lord. The word means that God heard her prayer.

When the time came for Elkanah and his family to go up, after their custom, to Shiloh, Hannah went not up with them, for she said, I will not go up till the child be weaned; and then will I bring him, that he may appear before the Lord and abide in his house all the days of his life.

So Hannah abode at home till she had weaned her son Samuel. After she had weaned him she took him up with her to Shiloh, to the tabernacle and brought the child to Eli. And Hannah said, Oh, my lord, as thy soul liveth, I am the woman that stood here near to thee, when thou wast sitting, as now, upon thy throne, and prayed unto the Lord. For this child I prayed; and the Lord hath given me my petition which I asked of him. Therefore also I have lent him to the Lord; as long as he liveth he shall be lent to the Lord.

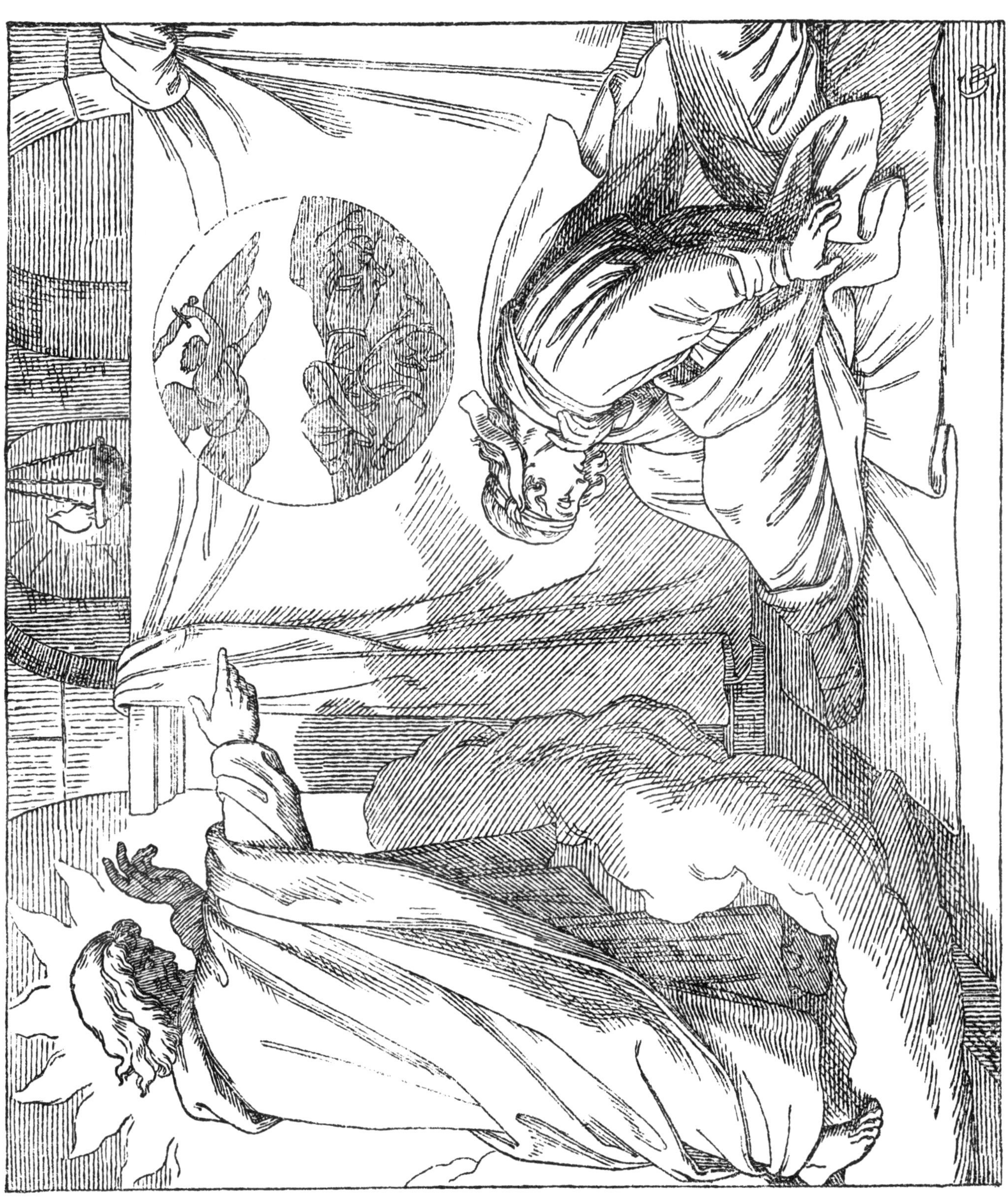

The Call of Samuel

And the Lord came to Samuel by night and called Samuel! Samuel! And Samuel felt the presence of the Lord, and answered, Speak; for thy servant heareth. And the Lord said: Behold, I will do a thing in Israel, which whosoever heareth both his ears shall tingle. In that day I will put over against Eli all that I have spoken concerning his house. When I begin, I will also make an end. For I have told him that I will judge his house forever for the inquity that he knoweth; because his sons brought a curse upon themselves, and he restrained them not. And therefore have I sworn unto the house of Eli that the iniquity of Eli's house shall not be purged with sacrifice nor offering forever.

And Samuel lay until the morning, when he opened the doors of the tabernacle. And he feared to show Eli the vision. Then Eli called him, and said, Samuel, my son! Samuel answered, Here am I. Then said Eli, What is the thing that the Lord hath said unto thee? I pray thee hide it not from me: God do so to thee, and more also, if thou hide from me any of the things which he said unto thee. Then Samuel told him all the words that he had heard. He hid nothing from him. And Eli said, It is the Lord; let him do what seemeth him good.

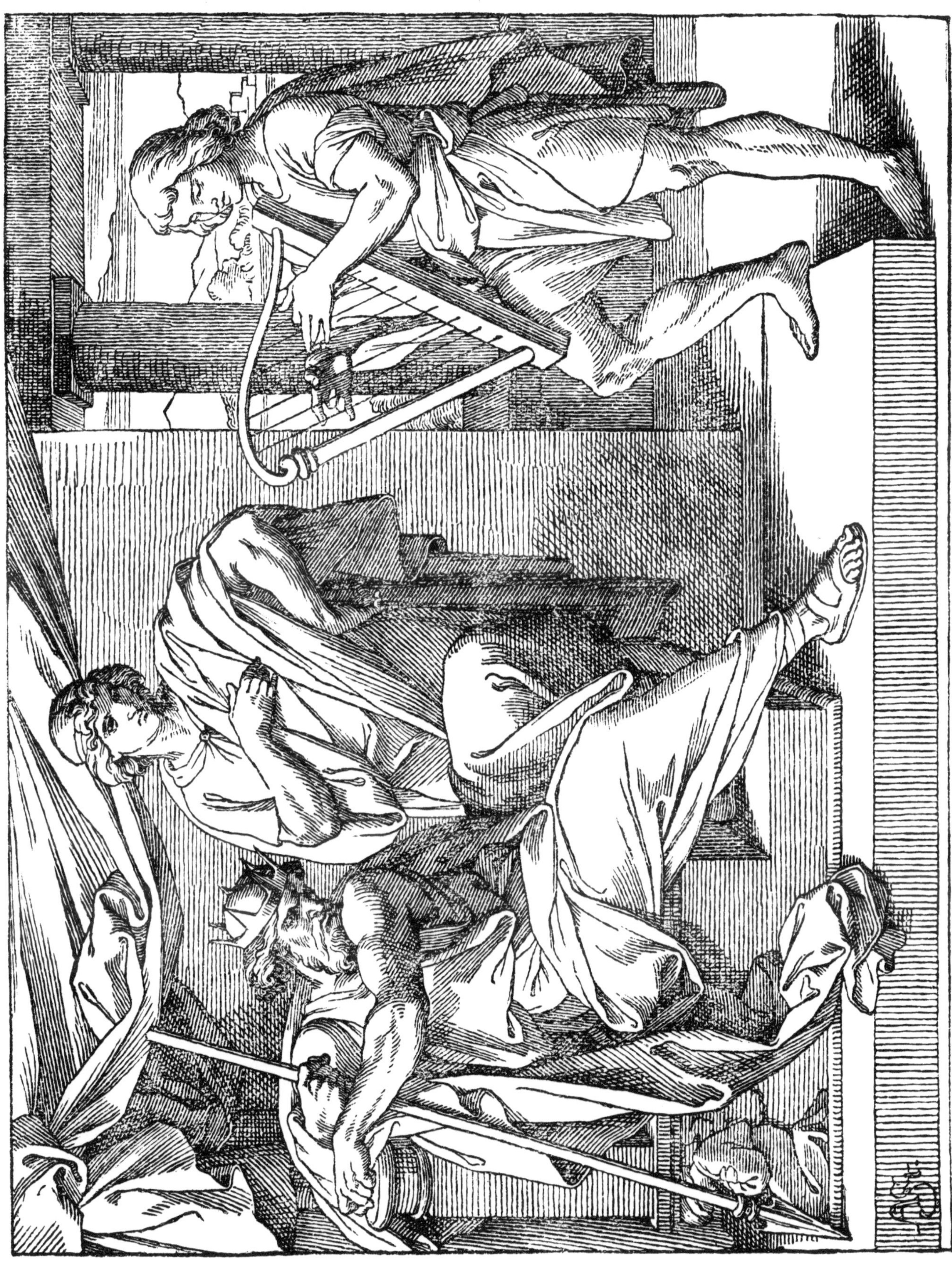

David Playing the Harp before Saul

An evil spirit from the Lord came to Saul and troubled him. And Saul's servants said unto him, let thy servants which are before thee seek out a man who is a skillful player upon a harp: and it shall come to pass, when the evil spirit of God is upon thee, that he shall play with his hand, and thou shalt be well.

Then Saul said unto his servants, Provide me now a man that can play well, and bring him to me. Then answered one of his servants, Behold, I have seen a son of Jesse the Bethlehemite, that is skilful in playing, and a valiant man, and prudent in speech; and also a comely person, and the Lord is with him.

Now this son of Jesse was named David. And the servants of Saul had heard how he had slain a lion and a bear while he kept his father's flocks; but they knew not that Samuel had anointed him to be king over Israel in the room of their master, for this thing had been done in secret.

So Saul sent messengers to Jesse, and said, Send me David thy son, who is with the sheep. Then Jesse took a donkey, and laded it with bread, and put on it also a skin of wine, and a kid, and sent them to Saul by David his son. And when the evil spirit came upon Saul, David took a harp, and played with his hand. Then Saul was refreshed and well, and the evil spirit departed from him.

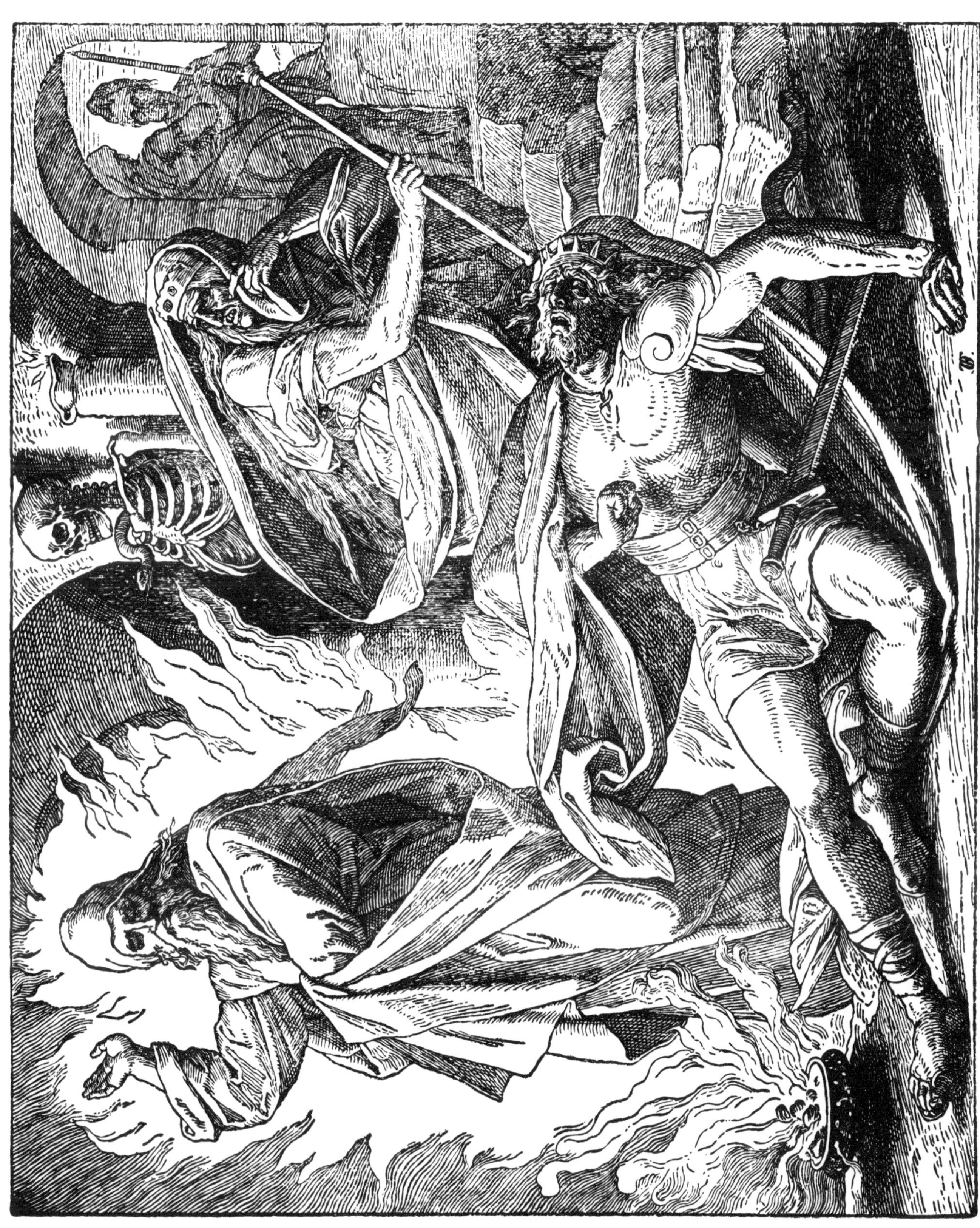

Saul and the Witch of Endor

When Samuel had been dead three years, the Philistines came up against the land of Israel, and pitched in Shunem, which is in the land of Issachar; and Saul gathered all Israel together, and pitched his camp in Gilboa. And when Saul saw the host of the Philistines, he was afraid, and his heart greatly trembled.

And when Saul inquired of the Lord, the Lord answered him not. Now before this, Saul had put away out of the land all that had familiar spirits, and all the wizards. Nevertheless, in his perplexity, he said unto his servants, Seek me now a woman that hath a familiar spirit, that I may go to her, and inquire of her.

And Saul's servants said to him, There is a woman that hath a familiar spirit at Endor. Then Saul disguised himself, and put on other raiment, and he went, and two other men with him, and they came to the woman by night. And he said to her, Help me by thy familiar spirit, and bring him up whom I shall name unto thee. The woman said unto him, Thou knowest what Saul hath done, how he hath cut off those that have familiar spirits, and wizards, out of the land: wherefore then layest thou a snare for my life, to cause me to die?

Then Saul sware to her by the Lord, saying, As the Lord liveth, there shall no punishment happen unto thee for this thing. Then said the woman, Whom shall I bring up unto thee? And he said, Bring me up Samuel. Then the woman used her incantations. But when she saw Samuel, she cried with a loud voice; and she spoke to Saul, saying, Why hast thou deceived me? For thou art Saul. The king said unto her, Be not afraid: what sawest thou? The woman answered, I saw the shape as of a god ascending out of the earth. Saul said, What form is he of?

The woman answered, An old man cometh up; and he is covered with a robe. And Saul perceived that it was Samuel, and he stooped with his face to the ground, and bowed himself. Then Samuel said,Why hast thou disquieted me, to bring me up? And Saul said, I am sore distressed; for the Philistines war against me, and God is departed from me, and answereth me no more, neither by the word of prophets, nor by dreams: therefore I have called thee, that thou mayest make known unto me what I shall do.

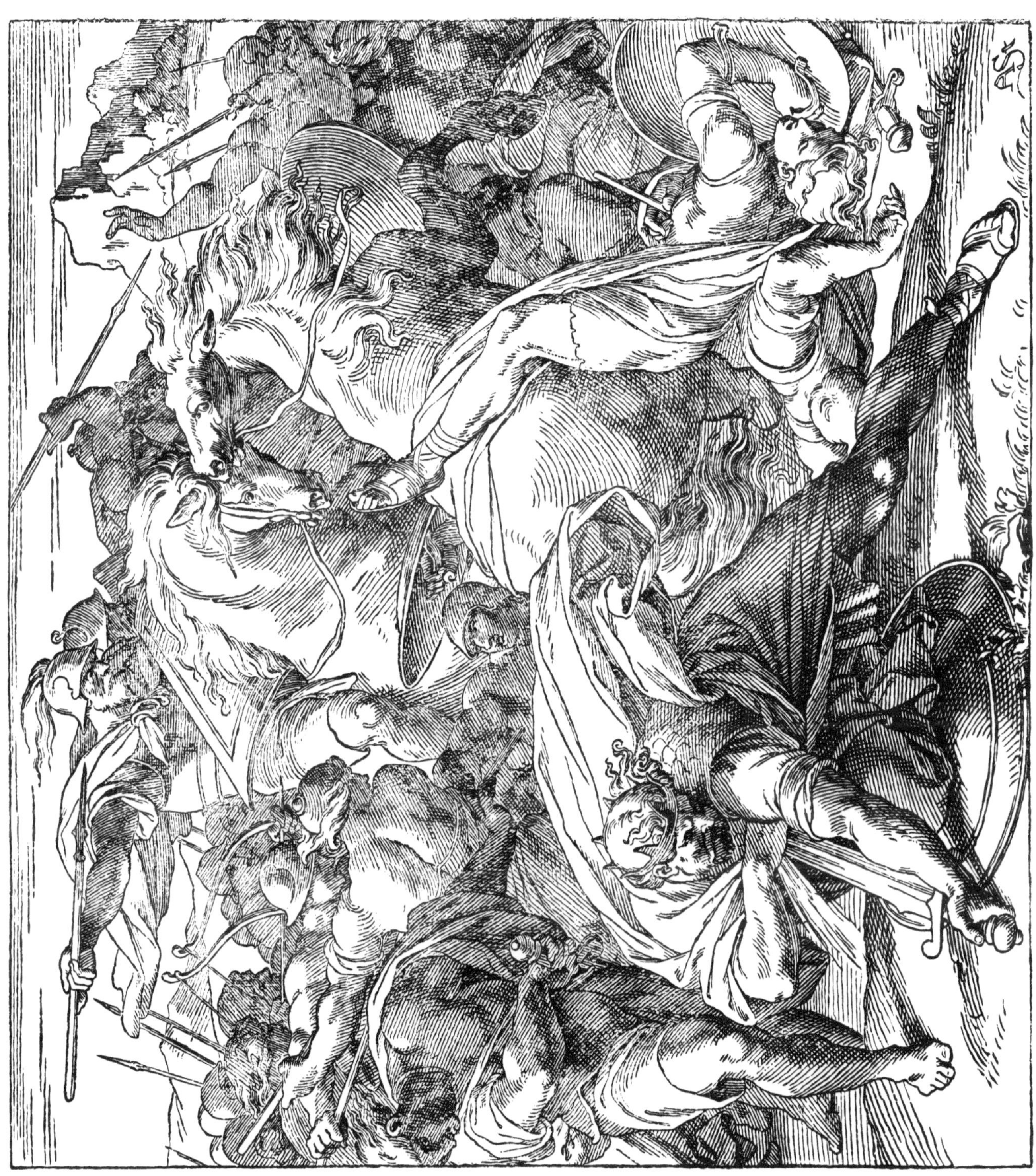

Saul Kills Himself by Falling on his Sword

The Israelites came down from Mount Gilboa, and pitched by the fountain that is in the valley of Jezreel. Then the Philistines fought with them; and Israel fled before the Philistines to Mount Gilboa, and many fell down slain upon the mount.

The Philistines followed hard upon Saul and his sons. His sons they slew, even Jonathan and Abinadab and Melchishua. And the battle went sore against Saul, for the archers shot at him and wounded him, none daring to come near to smite him with the sword or the spear; and Saul was sore afraid of the archers.

Then said Saul to his armor-bearer, Draw thy sword, and thrust me through therewith; lest these uncircumcised come and thrust me through, and mock my body when I am dead. But his armor-bearer would not, for he feared to slay the king. Therefore Saul took a sword and fell upon it. And when his armor-bearer saw that he was dead, he fell likewise upon his sword, and died with him. So Saul died, and his three sons, and his armor-bearer, and all the men that were with him, that same day together.

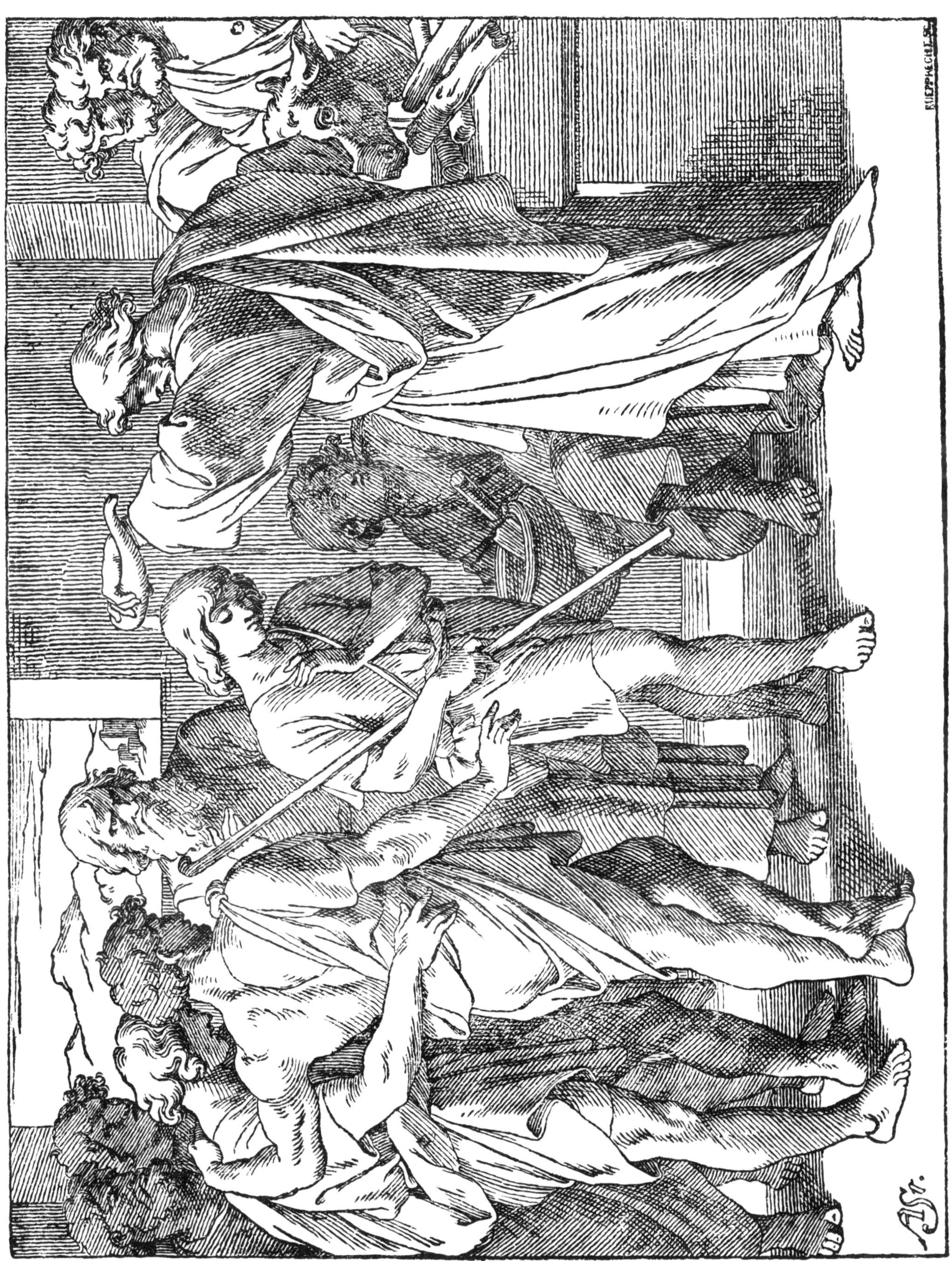

Samuel Anointing David at Bethlehem

In the days of King Saul there dwelt at Bethlehem, in the land of Judah, a certain man whose name was Jesse. This Jesse had eight sons and two daughters, and the youngest of his sons was David.

The Lord, being displeased with Saul, said to Samuel, Fill thine horn with oil, and go to the house of Jesse in Bethlehem: for I have provided me a king among his sons. So Samuel went. And the elders of Bethlehem, knowing that he and the king were not friends, said to him, Comest thou peaceably? And he said, Peaceably: I am come to sacrifice to the Lord; purify yourselves, and come to the sacrifice. He bade also Jesse and his sons purify themselves, and he invited them to the sacrifice.

And when they came, and he saw Eliab the eldest, and perceived how goodly and tall he was, he said, Surely the Lord's anointed is before him. But the Lord said, Look not on his countenance, nor on the height of his stature; because I have refused him: for the Lord seeth not as man seeth; for man looketh on the outward appearance, but the Lord looketh on the heart. Then Jesse made Abinadab, his second son, and then Shammah, his third son, pass before Samuel, and after these yet four others. But Samuel said, The Lord hath not chosen these.

He said again, Are all thy children here? Jesse answered, There remaineth yet the youngest, and he keepeth the sheep. Then Samuel said, Send and fetch him; for we will not sit down till he come. So Jesse sent for him. Now he was a youth, short of stature, his hair of a ruddy color, his eyes bright, and he was fair to look upon. And when he came, the Lord said to Samuel, This is he; arise, and anoint him. So Samuel anointed him in the midst of his brethren, and from that day the Spirit of the Lord came upon him.

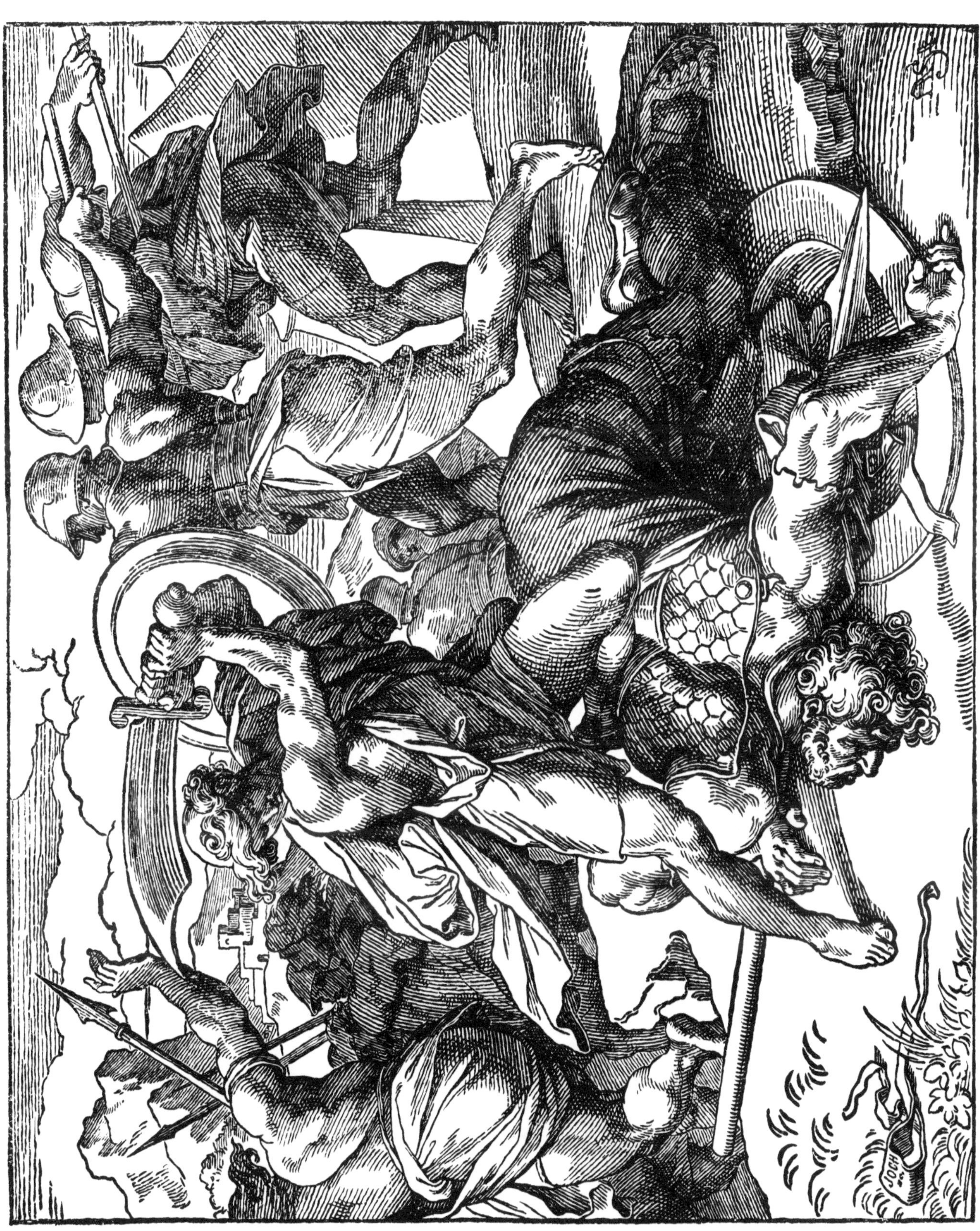

DAVID SLAYING GOLIATH

There came a champion from the camp of the Philistines named Goliath of Gath, whose height was over eight feet. And he was clad in a heavy coat of mail, with a helmet of brass upon his legs; and between his shoulders he carried a javelin of brass. The staff of his spear was like a weaver's beam, and the spear head weighed about seventeen pounds. And one bearing a shield went before.

And the man called to the men of Israel, Choose a man and send him to fight with me. If he be able to kill me, then will we be your servants; but if I prevail over him, and kill him, then shall ye serve us. But Saul and all Israel were dismayed at his words, for there was none that could match him in stature or in the strength of his armor. Forty days, day by day, did Golilath challenge the men of Israel.

Now the three eldest sons of Jesse had followed Saul to the camp of this battle. And one day Jesse said to David his son, go to thy brothers and see how they fare and bring back an answer from them. So David went and as he talked with his brothers, Goliath came forth, and cried as he was wont; and David heard his words. All the men of Israel fled at the sight of him, for they were sore afraid. But David said, Who is this Philistine that he should defy the armies of the living God? And the words that David had said were told to Saul, and Saul sent for him.

Then David said to Saul, Behold, thy servant will go and fight with him. Saul answered, Thou art not able to fight with this Philistine; for thou art but a youth, and he a man of war. But David said, I kept my father's sheep, and a bear came and took a lamb out of the flock; and I slew him; and as I returned to the flock, a lion met me; him also I slew. This Philistine shall fare as these, seeing that he hath defied the armies of the living God; for truly he that delivered me out of the paw of the lion, and out of the paw of the bear, will also deliver me out of the hand of this Philistine. So Saul said, Go, and the Lord be with thee. And Saul clad him in armor, and put a helmet upon his head, and gave him a sword. But David had never used such things, and when he tried to go in them, he could not. So he put them off, and took his staff in his hand, and chose five smooth stones out a brook in the valley, putting them in his shepherd's wallet, and so went, having his sling in his hand, and drew near to the Philistine.

The Philistine also came on, and drew near to David; and when he looked about, and saw David, he despised him, for he was but a youth and of a fair countenance. And he said to David, Am I a dog that thou comest to me with staves? Come near, and I will give thy flesh unto the fowls of the air and the beasts of the field. Then said David to the Philistine, Thou comest to me with a sword, a spear, and a shield; but I come to thee in the name of the Lord God of Israel. This day will the Lord deliver thee into mine hand; and I will smite thee, and take thine head; and I will give the carcases of the host of the Philistines to the beasts of the field and the fowls of the air, that all the earth may know that there is a God in Israel.

And when Goliath drew near, David ran to meet him; and he put his hand in his wallet, and took thence and threw it, and smote the Philistine on the forehead; and the stone sank in, and he fell on his face to the earth. So David prevailed over Goliath with a sling and a stone. But, because he had no sword, he ran and stood on the Philistine, and drawing the man's sword out of its sheath, smote off his head therewith.

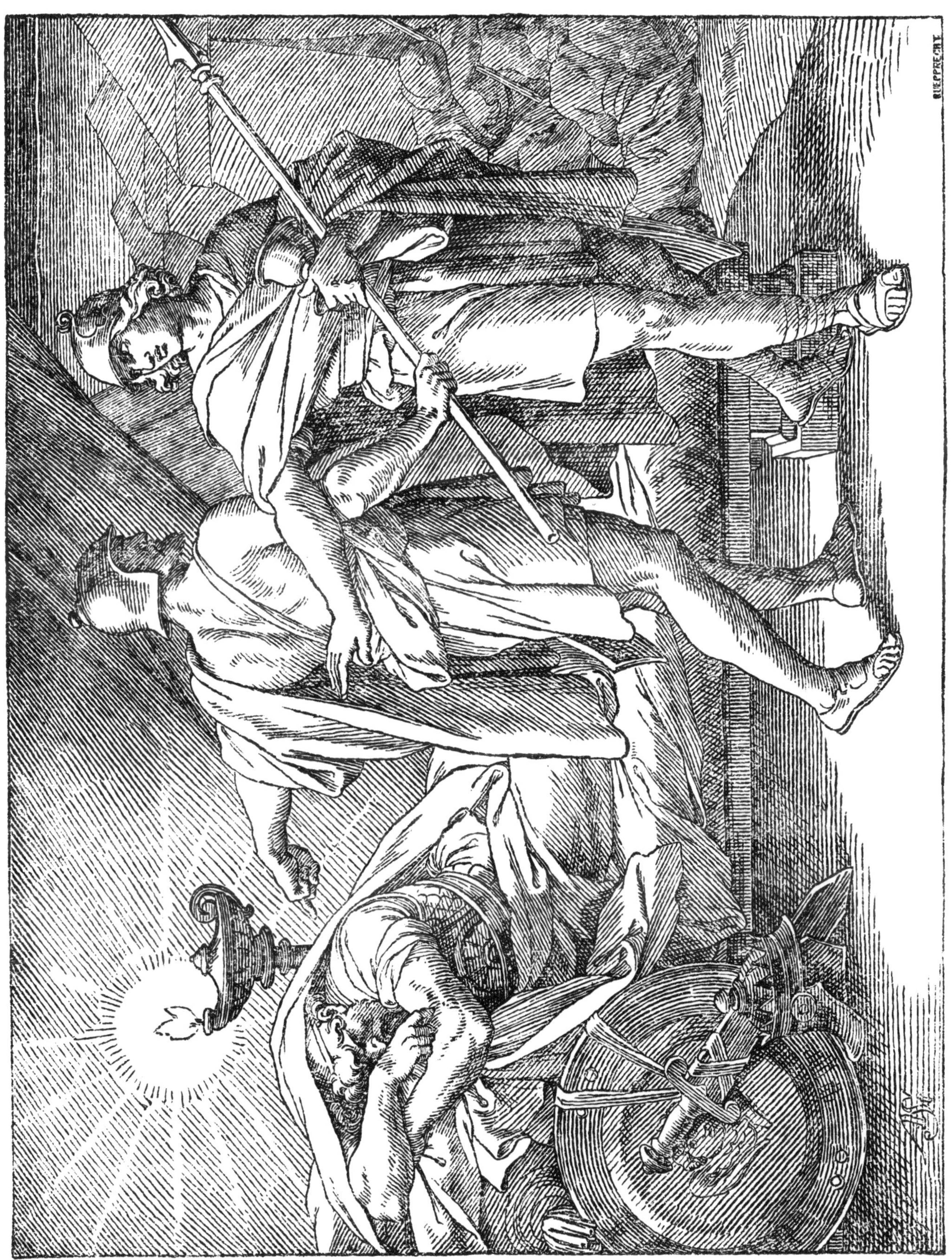

David Spares the Sleeping Saul

Saul lay sleeping behind some wagons, and his spear was stuck in the ground by his bolster. Then Abishai said to David, God hath delivered thine enemy into thine hand. Let me now smite him with the spear into the earth; I will not smite him a second time.

But David said to Abishai, Destroy him not; for who can stretch forth his hand against the Lord's anointed, and be guiltless? The Lord shall smite him; or his day will come to die; or he shall descend into the battle and perish; but God forbid that I should stretch my hand against him.

Then he took the spear and the cruse of water from Saul's bolster. After this the two got them away; and no man saw it or knew it, for a deep sleep from the Lord had fallen upon them all.

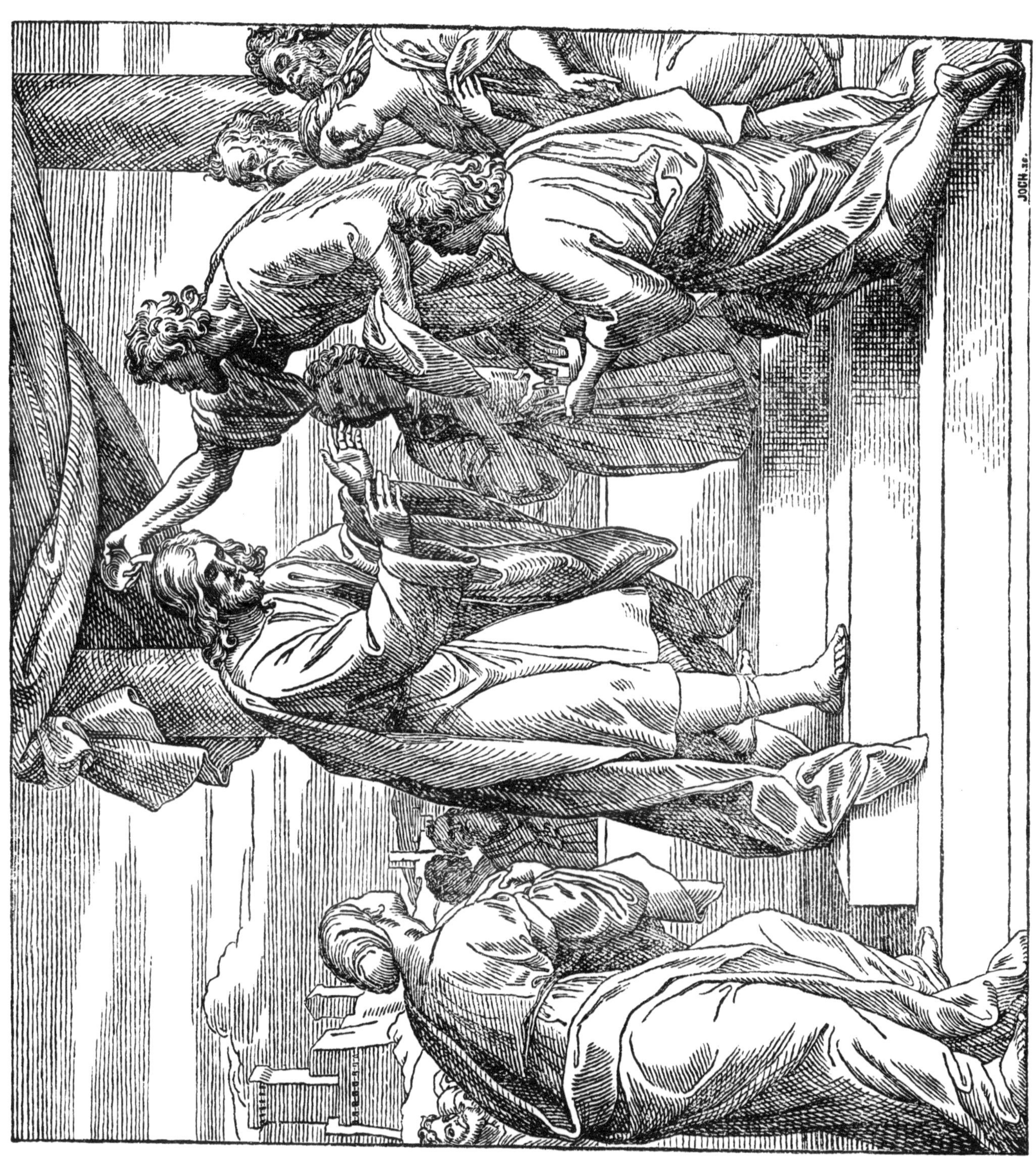

David Anointed King Over Israel

Saul and his sons had fallen on Mount Gilboa, and the army of Israel was destroyed; then those who dwelt in the plains of Jezreel and by the borders of Jordan fled from their cities, and the Philistines came and dwelt in them. Then the men, seeing that they wanted a leader, chose David to be their king.

Then came all the tribes of Israel to David in Judah, saying, Behold, we are thy bone and thy flesh. In time past, when Saul was king over us, thou wast he that leddest out Israel and broughtest them back. And the Lord said to thee, Thou shalt feed my people Israel, and be a captain over Israel.

Then David the king made a covenant with them in Hebron before the Lord, and they anointed him king over Israel. And after he was anointed they abode with David three days eating and drinking, for their brethren that dwelt near to the city had prepared a great store of good things for them; bringing food on camels and mules and oxen, even meal, and cakes of figs, and bunches of raisins, and wine, and oil, and oxen, and sheep abundantly; for there was joy in Israel.

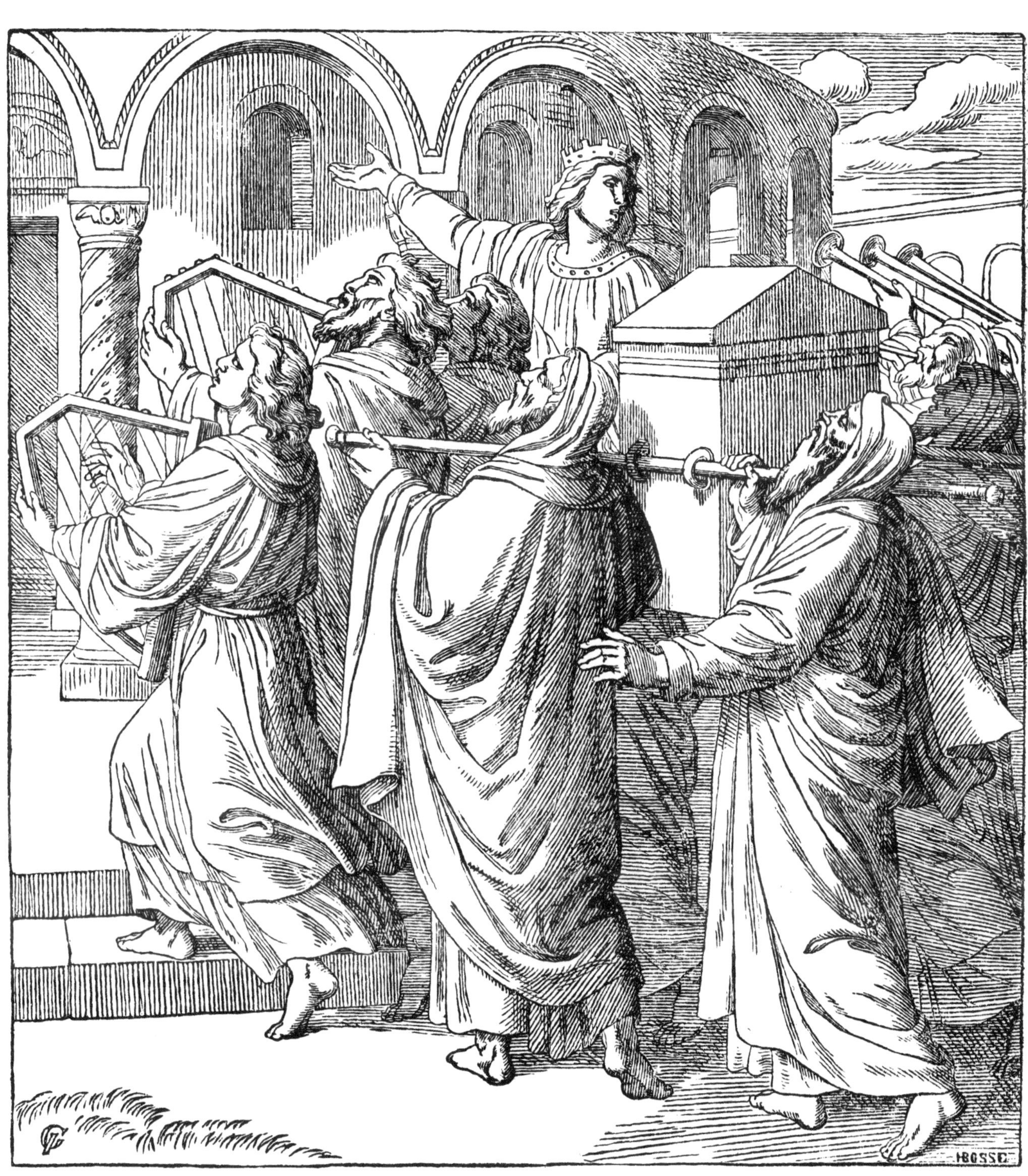
HBOSSE

The Ark Brought Into the Temple by Solomon

In the fourth year of his reign did Solomon begin to build the house of the Lord; and in the eleventh year of his reign he finished it. Above the topmost story were windows in the walls of the house, to light fathers that they might bring up the ark of the covenant out of the city of David. There was nothing in the ark save the two tables of stone which Moses had put there in Horeb, when the Lord made a covenant with the children of Israel, when they came out of the land of Egypt. So the priests took up the ark of the Lord, and the tabernacle that Moses had made in the wilderness, and all the holy vessels that were in the tabernacle, and brought them into the Holy Place.

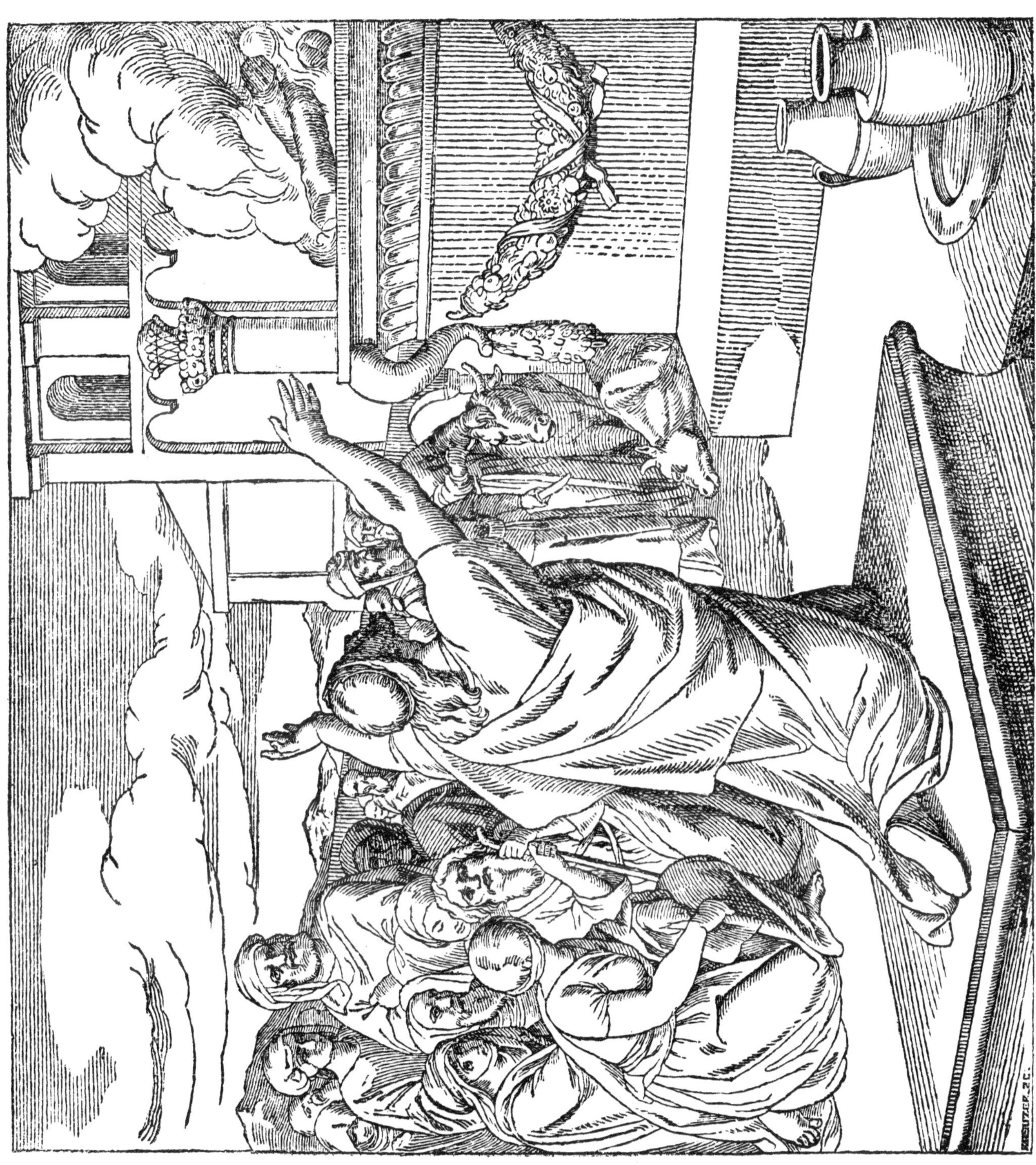

Solomon Dedicating the Temple

In the twelfth year of his reign, at the time of the Feast of Tabernacles, King Solomon dedicated the house which he had built. He stood before the brazen altar in the court of the priests on a platform of brass, that he might be seen of the people; and he knelt upon his knees, and spread forth his hands and prayed to the Lord God of Israel, saying:

Lord God of Israel, there is no God like thee, in heaven above, or on earth beneath, who keepest covenant and mercy with thy servants that walk before thee with all their heart; who hast kept with thy servant David my father that thou didst promise him; thou spakest also with thy mouth, and hast fulfilled it with thine hand, as it is this day, Now, therefore, keep thy promise that thou promisedst him, saying, There shall not fail thee a man to sit on the throne of Israel; so that thy children take heed to their way, that they walk before me, as thou hast walked before me.

Will God indeed dwell on the earth? Behold the heavens cannot contain thee; how much less this house that I have builded. Yet have thou respect unto my prayer, that thine eyes may be open towards this house day and night, even towards the place of which thou hast said, my name shall be there. Hearken thou to the supplication of thy servant, and of thy people Israel, when they shall pray toward this place; and hear thou in heaven thy dwelling place; and when thou hearest, forgive.

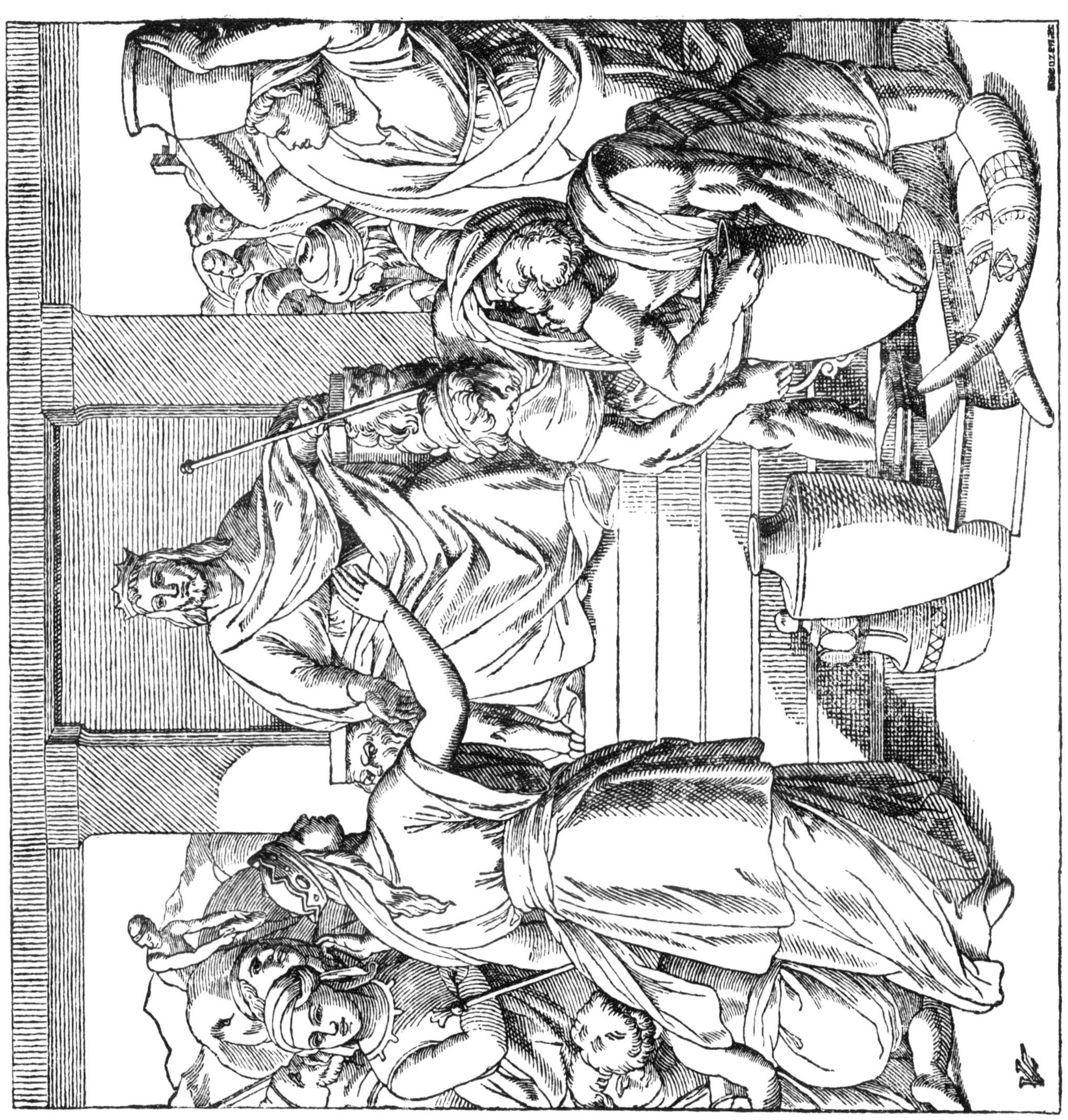

The Queen of Sheba Visiting Solomon

When the Queen of Sheba heard of the fame of Solomon, and how the Lord had given him great wisdom, she came to prove him with hard questions. With a very great train did she come to Jerusalem, with camels that bore spices, and very much gold, and precious stones. And when she came to Solomon, she communed with him of all that was in her heart. And Solomon told her all her questions: there was not anything hid from the queen that he told her not.

And when the Queen of Sheba had seen all the wisdom of Solomon, and the house that he had built, and the meat of his table, and the sitting of his servants, and the attendance of his ministers, and their apparel, and his cupbearers, and how he went in his state to the house of the Lord, there was no more spirit in her.

And she said to the king, It was a true report that I heard in my own land of thy acts and thy wisdom. Howbeit I believed not the words till I came, and mine eyes had seen it; and, behold, the half was not told me; thy wisdom and prosperity exceedeth the fame which I heard. Happy are thy men, happy are these thy servants, which stand continually before thee, and hear thy wisdom. Blessed be the Lord thy God, which delighted in thee, to set thee on the throne of Israel: because the Lord loved Israel forever, therefore did he set thee on the throne, to do judgment and justice.

And she gave the king one hundred and twenty talents of gold, and of spices very great store, and precious stones: there came no more such abundance of spices as these which the Queen of Sheba gave to Solomon.

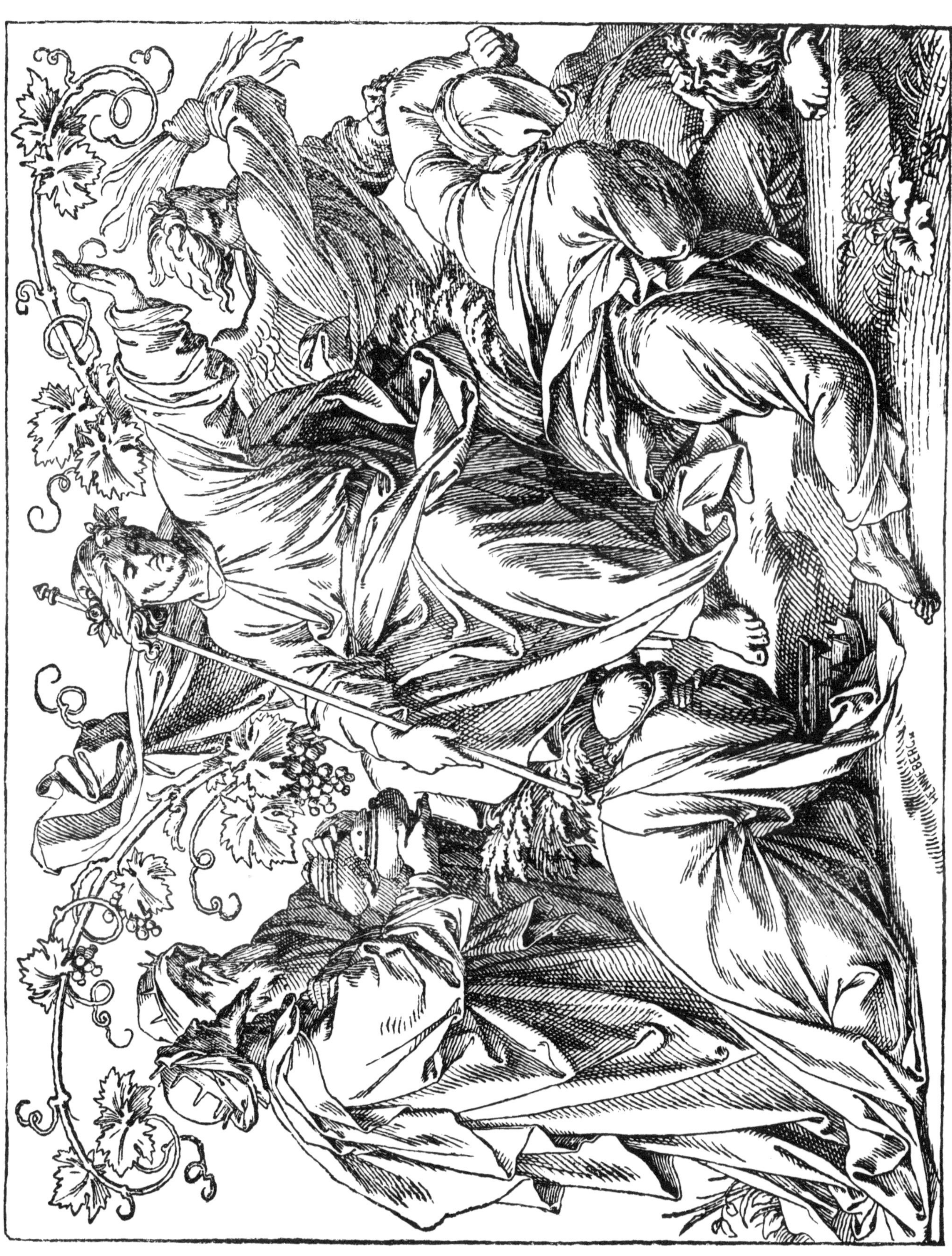

Kings Bringing Gifts to Solomon

All the countries round about sought to Solomon, to hear his wisdom, which God put in his heart; and they brought every man his present, vessels of silver, and vessels of gold, and garments, and armor, and spices, and horses, and mules.

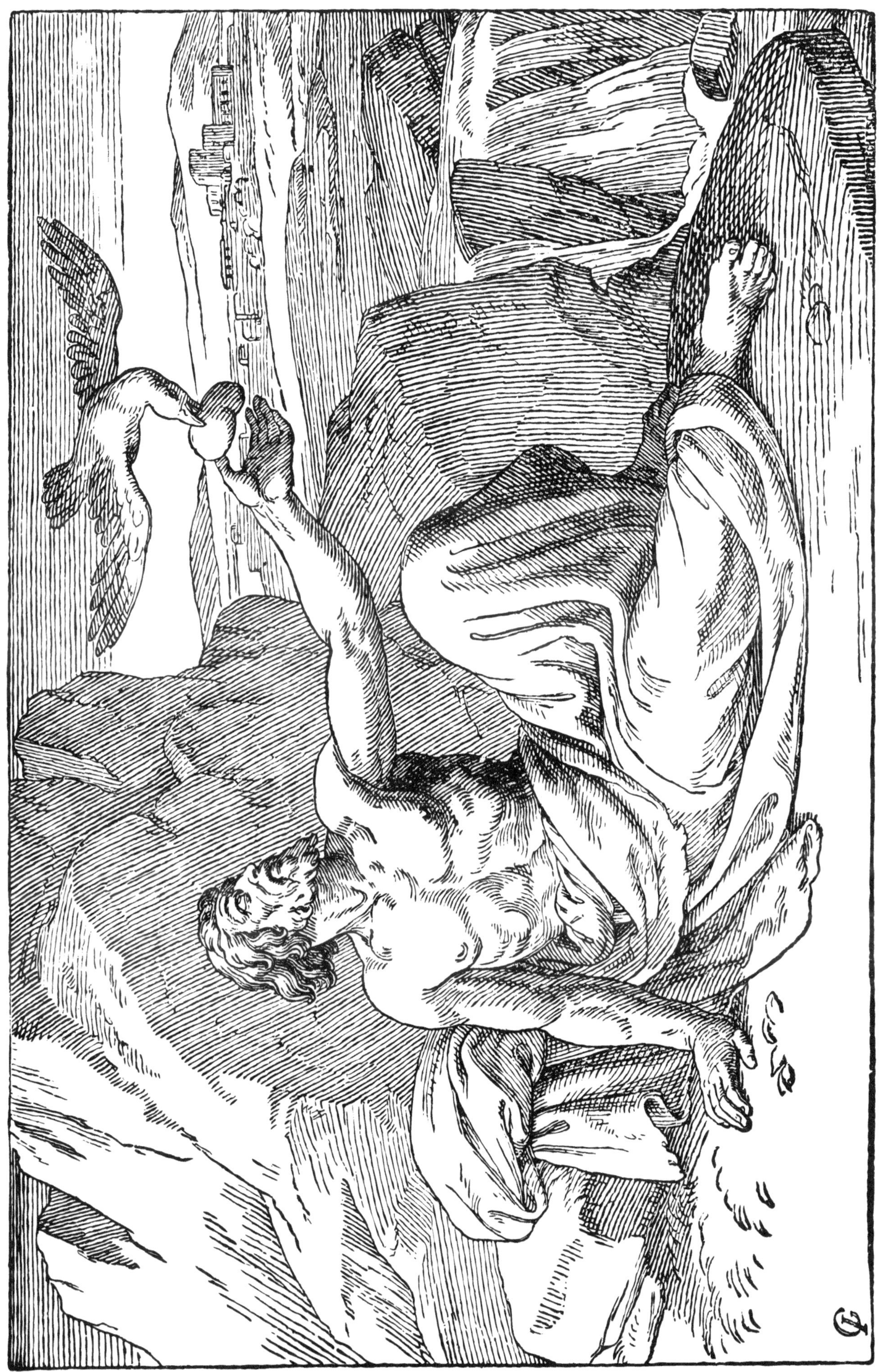

Elijah Fed by Ravens

Elijah was concealed, for the word of the Lord came to him, saying, Get thee hence, and turn thee eastward, and hide thee by the watercourse of Cherith, that floweth into Jordan. And it shall be that thou shalt drink of the brook; and I have commanded the ravens to feed thee there. So he went, and did according to the word of the Lord; for he dwelt by the watercourse of Cherith that floweth into Jordan. And the ravens brought him bread and flesh in the morning, and bread and flesh in the evening; and he drank from the watercourse.

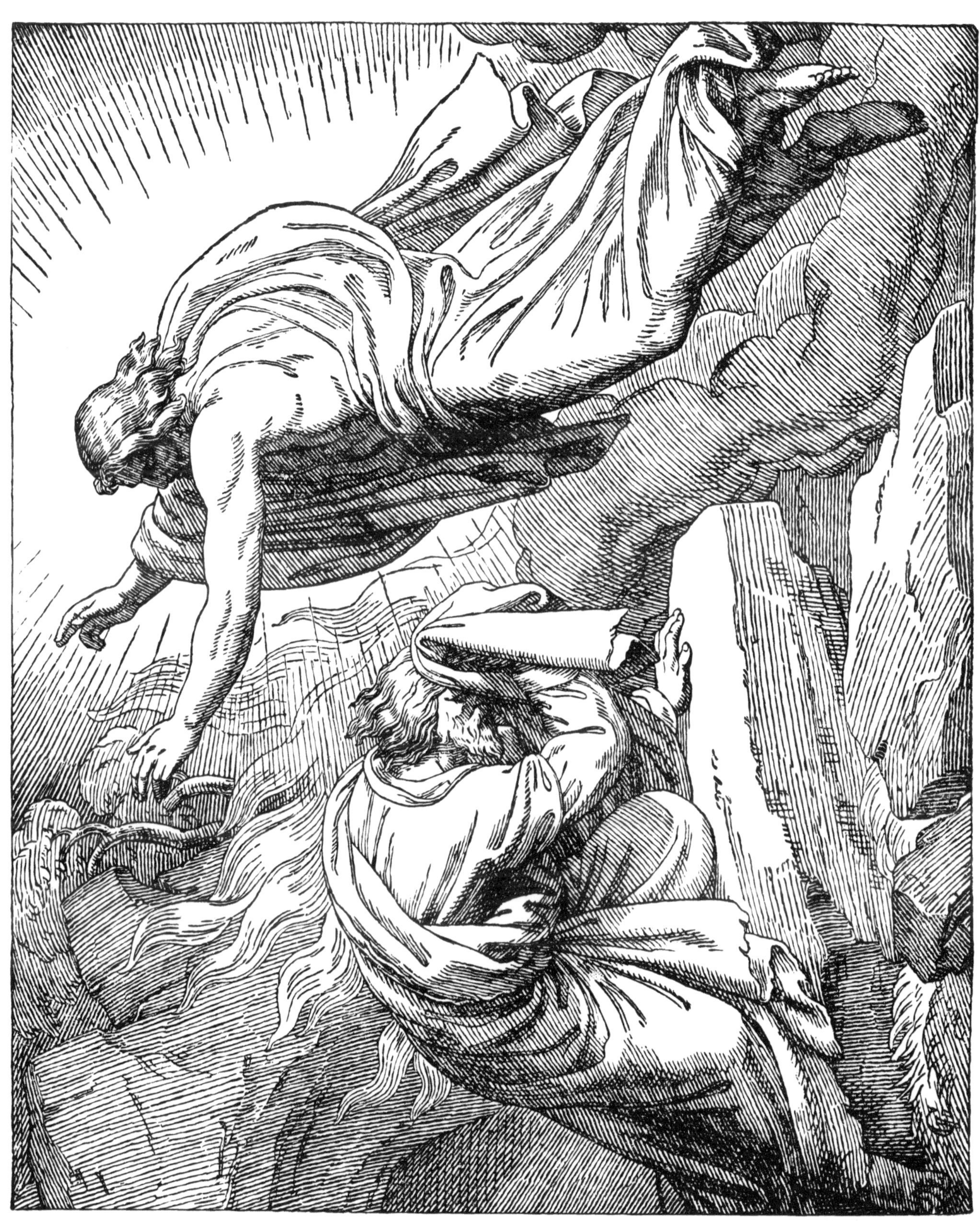

Elijah at the Mouth of the Cave

Elijah came to Horeb, the mount of God. And a great and strong wind rent the mountains, and broke the rocks in pieces before the Lord; but the Lord was not in the wind. And after the wind was an earthquake; but the Lord was not in the earthquake. And after the earthquake a fire; but the Lord was not in the fire. And after the fire, a still small voice.

When Elijah heard the voice, he wrapped his face in his mantle, and went out and stood in the mouth of the cave. And there came a voice to him, and said, What doest thou here, Elijah?

And he said, I have been very jealous for the Lord God of hosts: because the children of Israel have forsaken thy covenant, thrown down thine altars, and slain the prophets with the sword; and only I am left; and they seek my life to take it away.

Then the Lord said unto him, Go, return on thy way to the wilderness of Damascus. Thou shalt go and anoint Hazael to be king over Syria; and Jehu the son of Nimshi shalt thou anoint to be king over Israel; and Elisha the son of Shaphat, of Abelmeholah, shalt thou anoint to be a prophet in thy room. And it shall come to pass that him that escapeth the sword of Hazael shall Jehu slay; and him that escapeth the sword of Jehu shall Elisha slay. But know that I will have seven thousand in Israel, all the knees which have not bowed to Baal, and all the mouths which have not kissed him. So Elijah departed from Horeb, and he journeyed to the wilderness of Damascus.

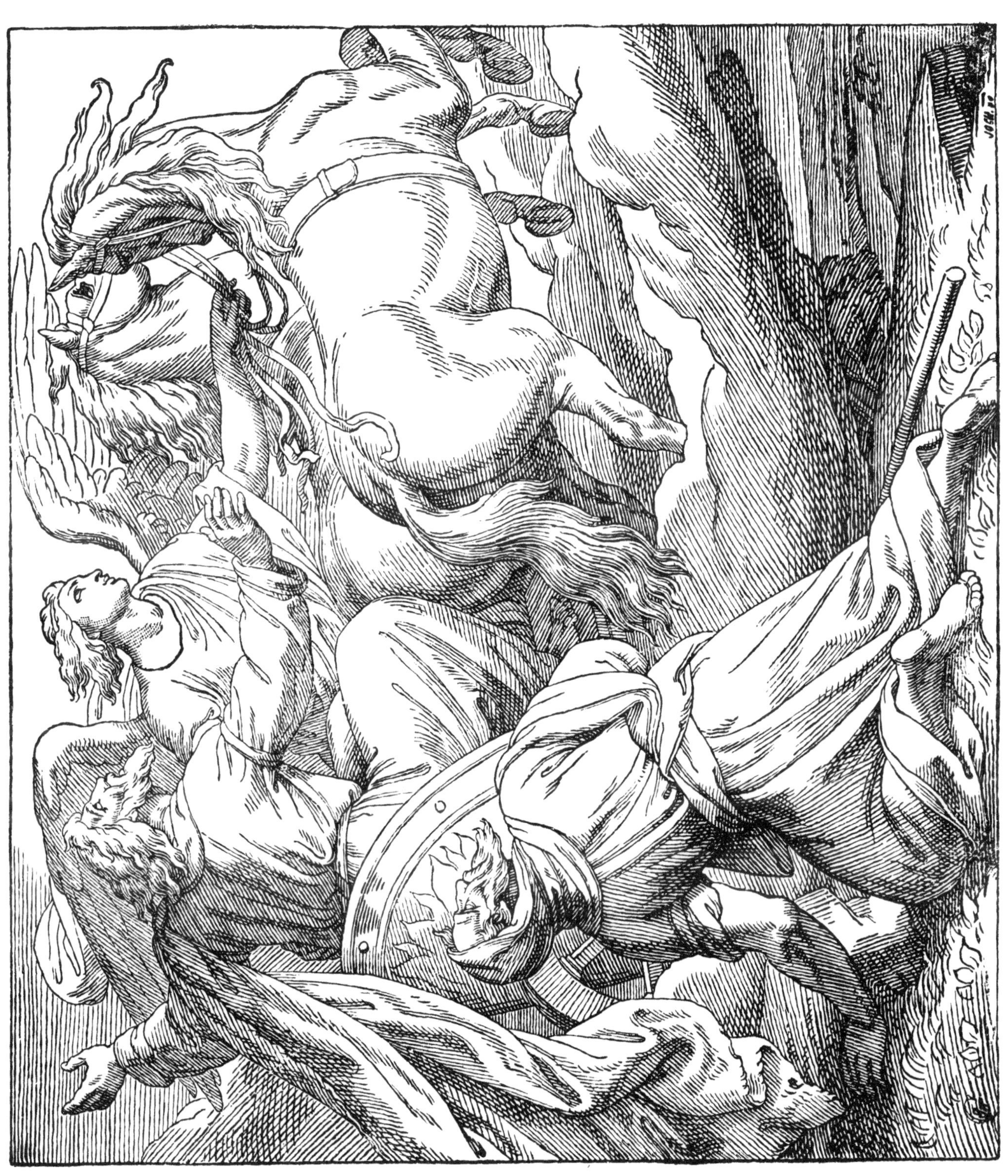

Elijah Taken Up into Heaven

When the Lord would take Elijah up into heaven, he went with Elisha, who ministered unto him. And they two went on to Jordan. And fifty men of the school of the prophets went and stood to view afar off. Then Elijah took his mantle, and rolled it up till it was as a rod, and smote the waters therewith; and they were divided hither and thither, so that they two went over on dry ground.

And when they had gone over, Elijah said to Elisha, Ask what I shall do for thee, when I shall be taken away from thee. Elisha said, I pray thee, let a double portion of thy spirit rest upon me. Elijah said, Thou hast asked a hard thing: if thou see me taken from thee, it shall be so unto thee; but if not, it shall not be so. And as they still went on and talked, behold there appeared a chariot of fire and horses of fire, and parted them both asunder; and Elijah went up by a storm into the sky.

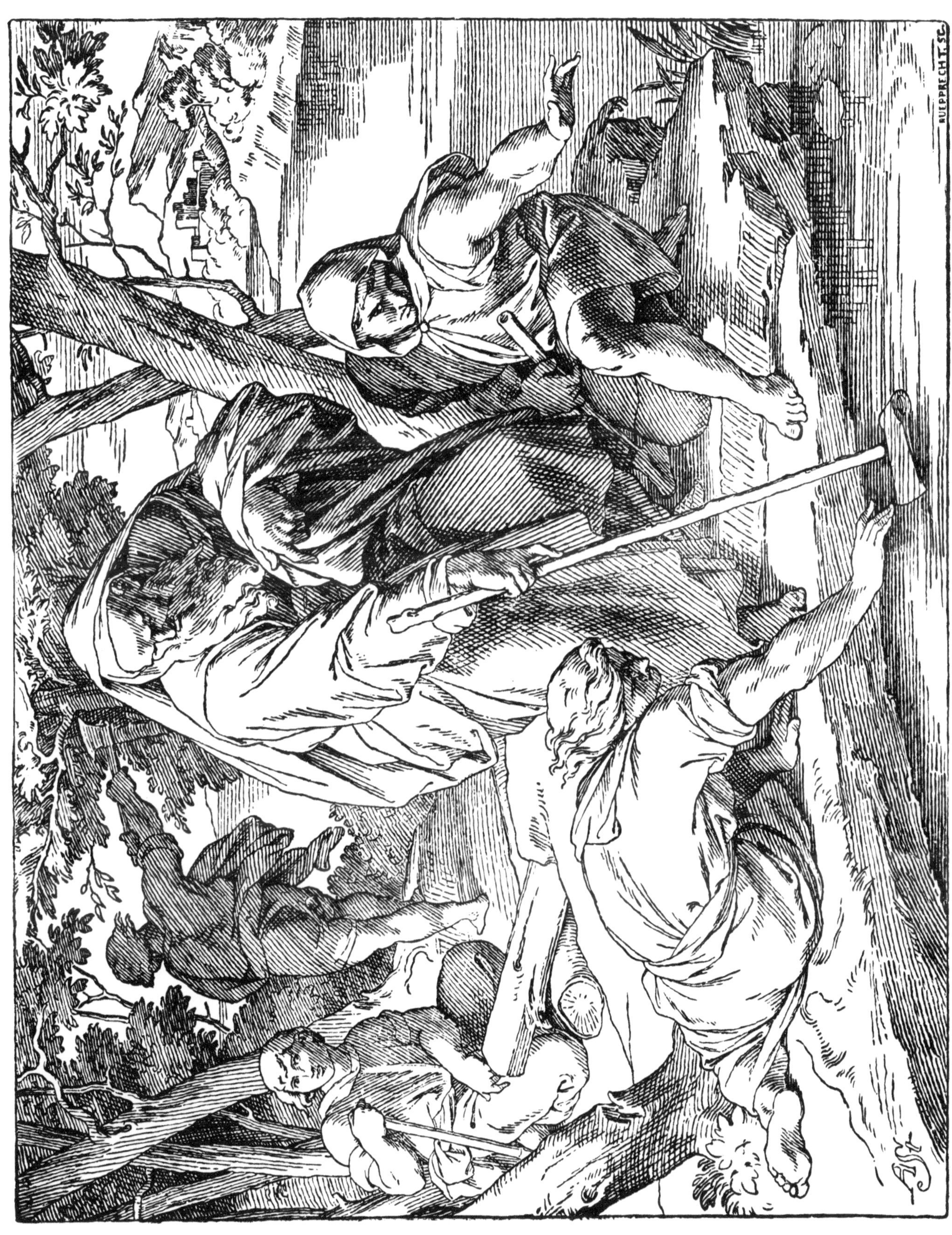

Elisha Causing Iron to Swim

The young men of the school of the prophets that was at Jericho said to Elisha, The place where we dwell is too narrow for us. Let us go unto Jordan, and take thence every man a beam, and let us make a place where we may dwell. Elisha answered, Go ye. One of the young men said, Consent to go with thy servants. And he answered, I will go.

So he went with them. And when they came to Jordan they cut down the wood. And as one was lopping a beam, the iron of the axe fell into the water, and the man cried out, Alas, master for it was borrowed. The man of God said, Where fell it? And when the man showed him the place, he cut down a stick and cast it in thither, and the iron did swim. Then he said to the man, Take it up to thee. And the man put out his hand and took it.

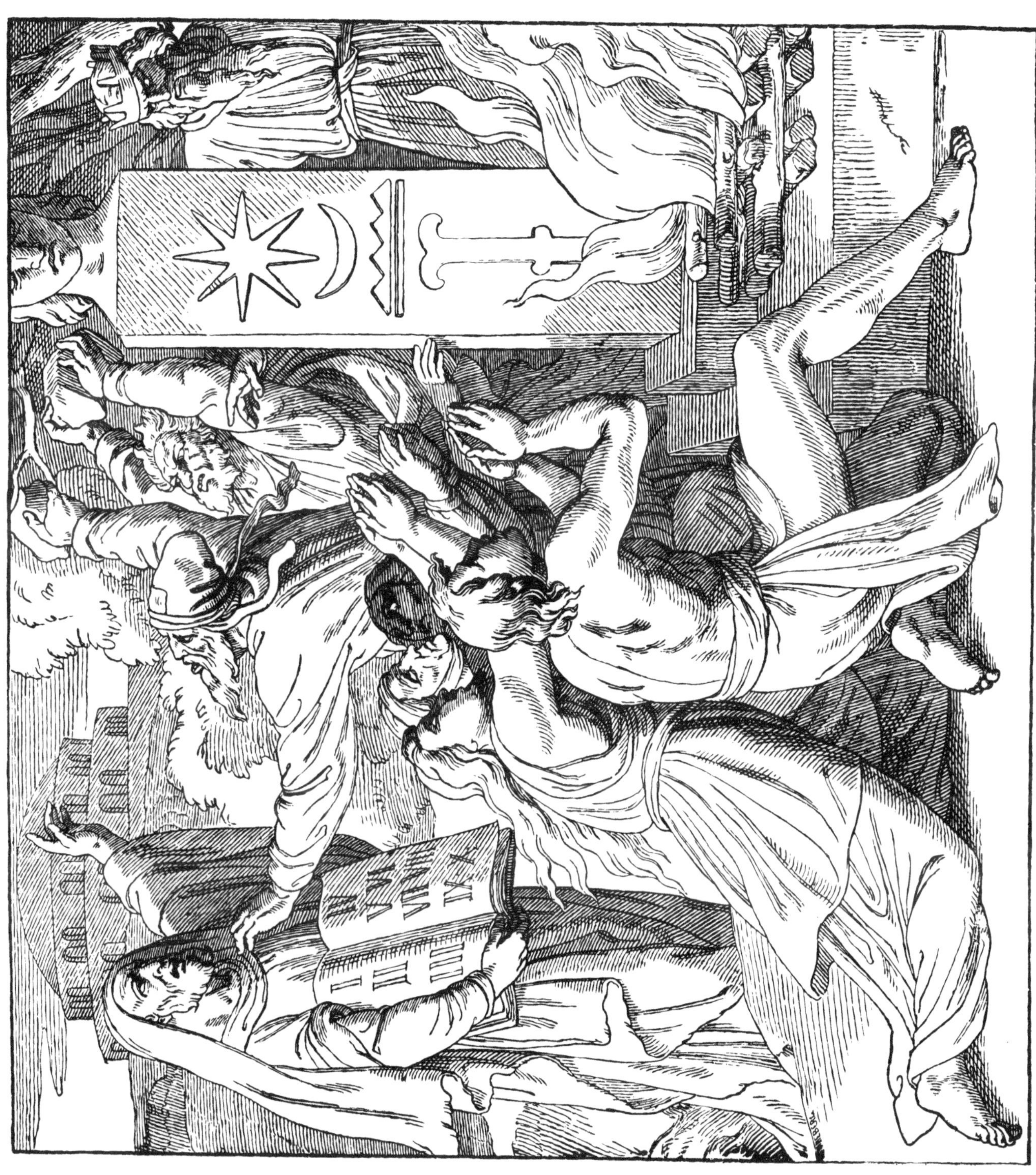

The Stoning of Zechariah

In the days of Elisha, when Joash was king of Judah, Zechariah, a good man, was high priest. He saw the idolatry of the people and prophesied against them, saying, Why transgress ye the commandments of the Lord, that ye cannot prosper? Because ye have forsaken the Lord, he hath also forsaken you.

This so displeased the king that he commanded Zechariah to be stoned to death. The high priest's father, Jehoiada, had shown kindness to the king, but this did not prevent the king from slaying the high priest. Afterward the king's servants conspired against him for the blood he had shed, and slew him on his bed. They buried him in the city of David, but not in the sepulchres of the kings.

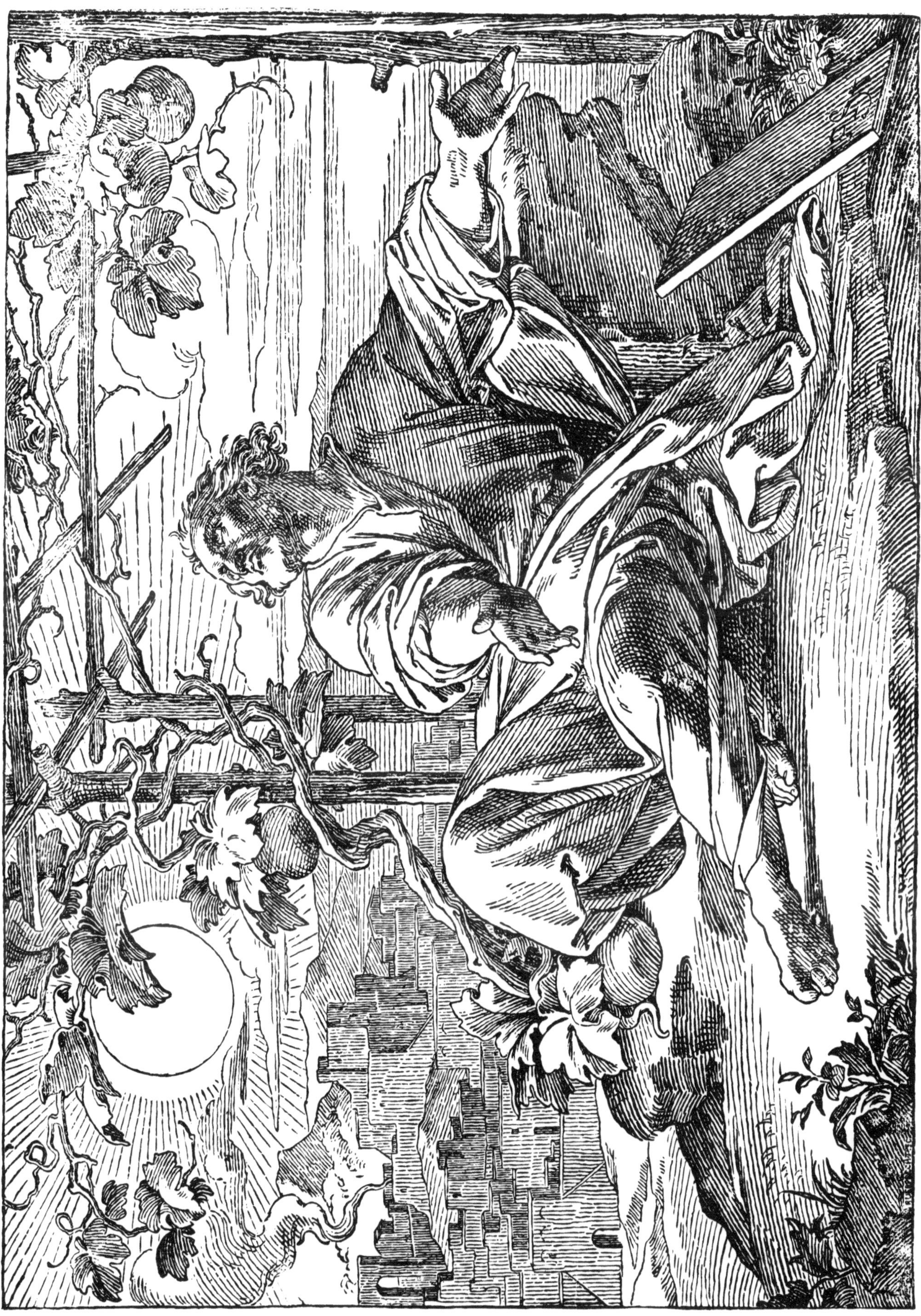

Jonah Sheltered by the Vine

While Jonah was watching the city of Nineveh, God bade a gourd grow up quickly to shelter him, and Jonah was very glad of its shade. But God prepared a worm to destroy the gourd in a night, so the next morning Jonah fainted from the heat, and then he grumbled because the gourd was gone. Then God said, You had pity on the gourd which came up in a night and perished in a night, why should I not spare that great city, Nineveh, with its large number of children and its innocent cattle? You fret at the loss of a worthless gourd, and you fret because I do not destroy a great city. You should rejoice in my mercy.

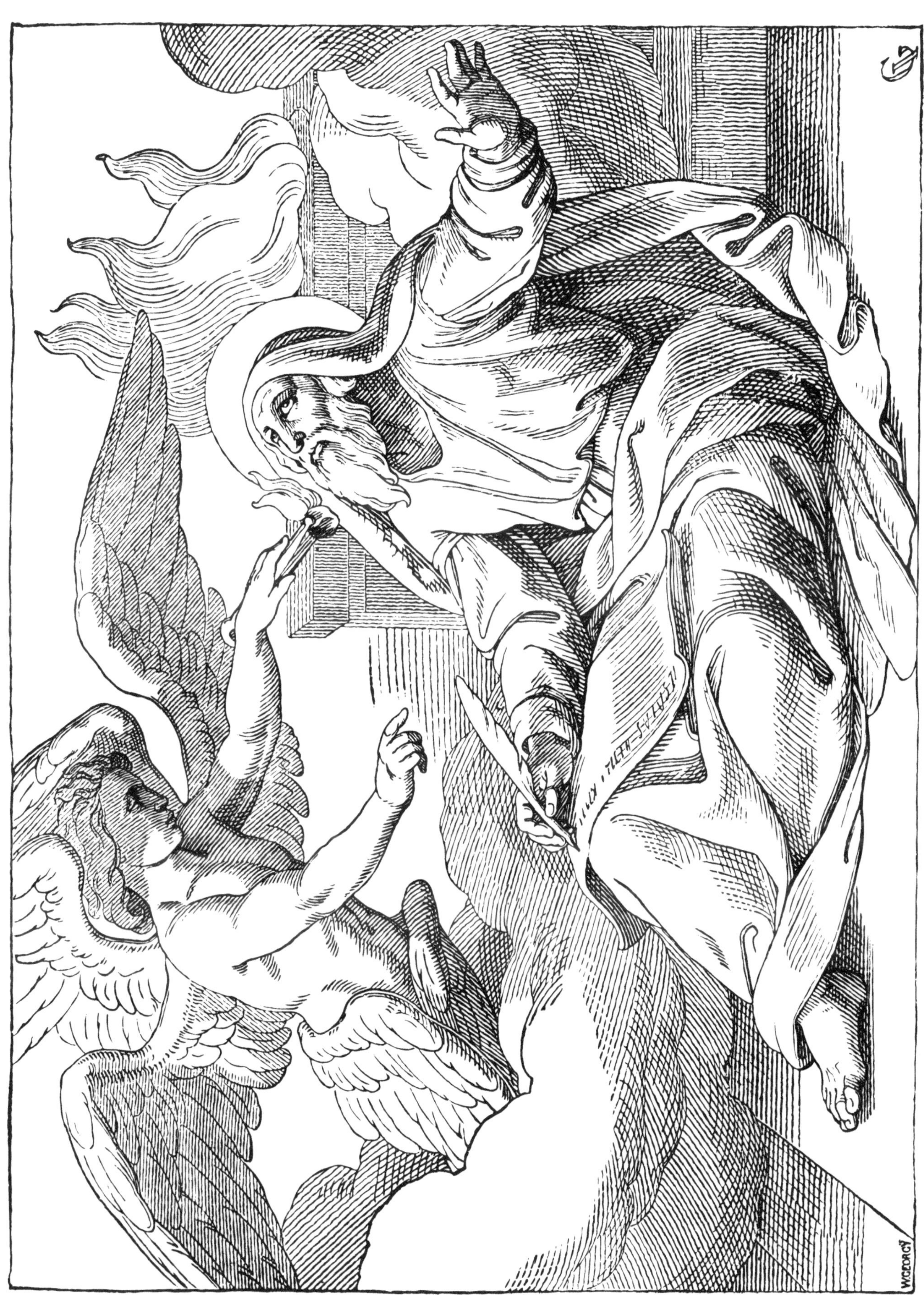

The Lips of Isaiah Touched with a Coal from the Altar

In the year that King Uzziah died, Isaiah saw the Lord sitting on a throne, and the train of his robe filled the temple. Above him stood the seraphim: each one had six wings; with two they covered their faces, and with two they covered their feet, and with two they did fly. And one cried to another, and said, Holy, holy, holy, is the Lord of hosts: the whole earth is full of his glory. And the posts of the door moved at the voice of their cries, and the house was filled with smoke.

Then said Isaiah, Woe is me! for I am undone; because I am a man of unclean lips, and I dwell in the middle of a people of unclean lips: for my eyes have seen the King, the Lord of hosts. Then flew one of the seraphim having a live coal in his hand, which he had taken with tongs from off the altar: And he laid it on the mouth of Isaiah, and said, See, this has touched your lips; and your iniquity is taken away, and your sin is purged.

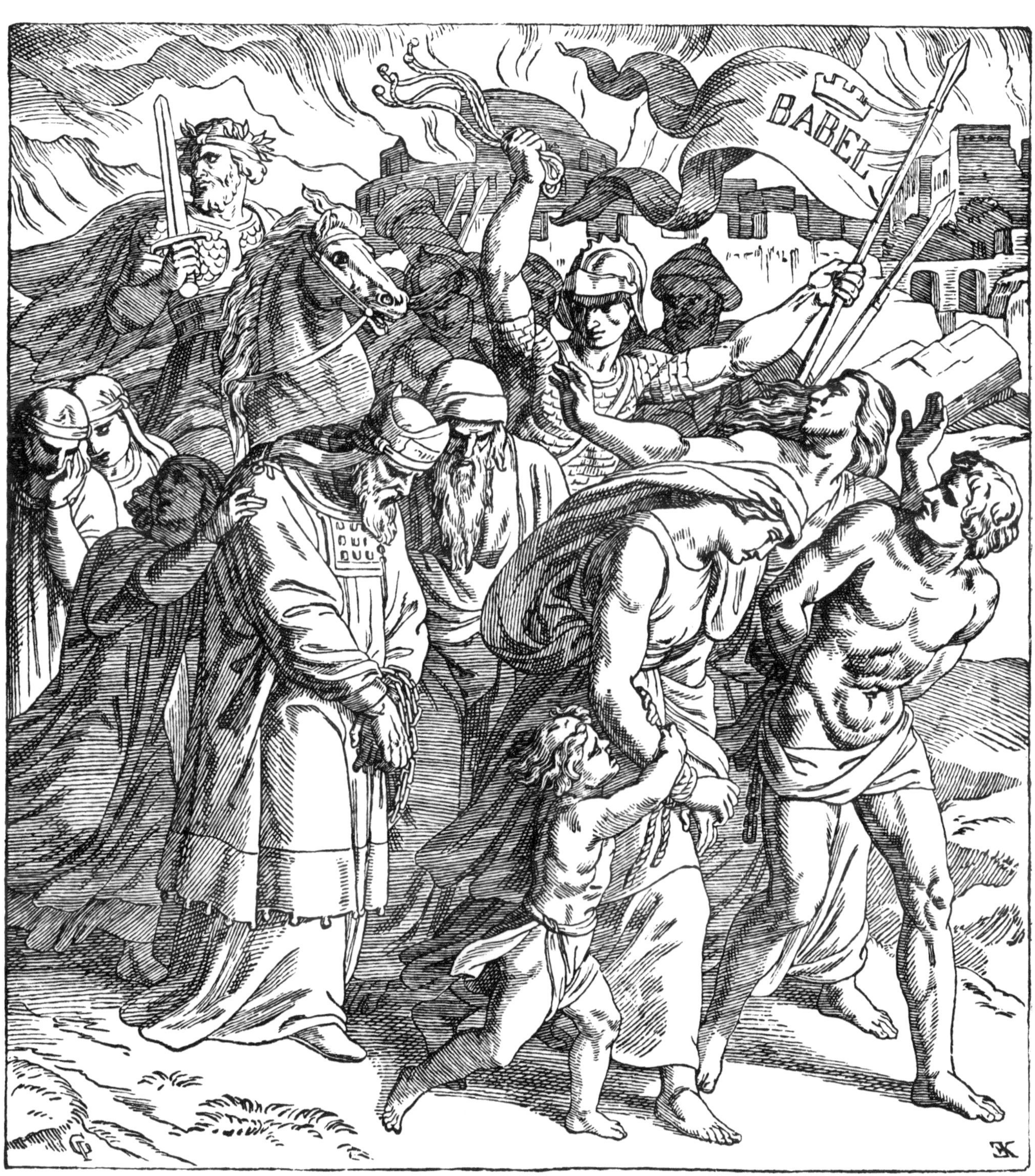
BABEL

The Jews Led into Captivity

The Israelites were divided into two kingdoms. Those who always had one of David's family for their king were called Jews, and only the other part of the nation were called Israelites. Both the Jews and the Israelites were constantly disobeying God and turning away from him. Again and again they built altars to worship false gods.

At last that thing happened to them which Moses had long ago told them would happen if they persisted in disobeying God. Their enemies came and destroyed their towns, and threw down their houses, and carried the people away into a strange land. This happened first to the Israelites.

Afterwards, Nebuchadnezzar, king of Babylon, came to Jerusalem and surrounded it with his soldiers. They broke down the walls of Jerusalem, and took it, and killed great numbers of the people. All the people who were not killed were carried away captives to Babylon.

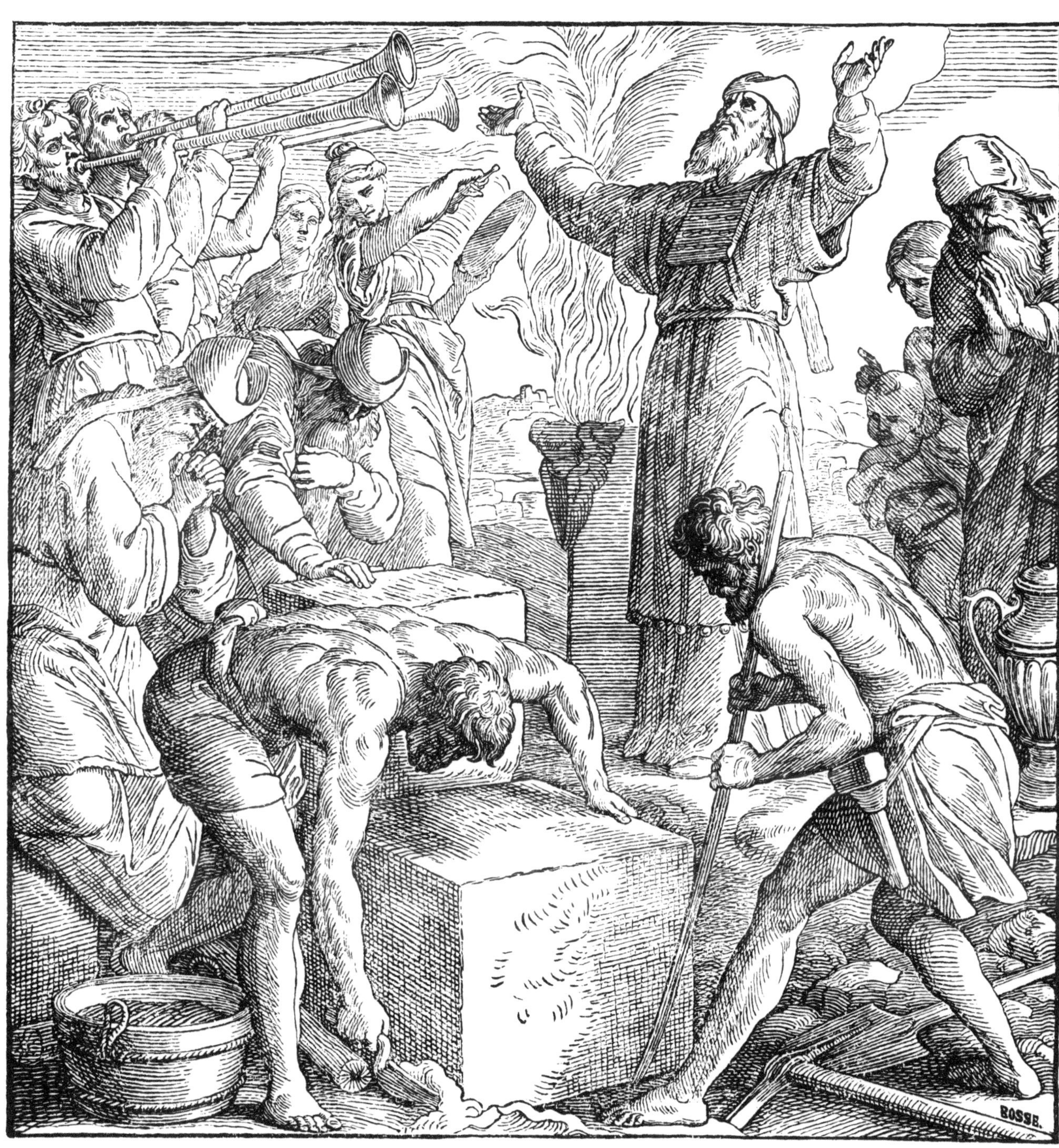
BOSSE.

Building a New Temple

Cyrus, king of Persia, when he had taken the city of Babylon, made proclamation throughout all his kingdom to this purpose: The Lord God of heaven hath given me all the kingdoms of the earth, and hath commanded me to build him a house at Jerusalem. Let all, therefore, that are of his people go up to Jerusalem and take their part in the building of this house. They that went up were forty-three thousand and upwards, and they had of men-servants and maid-servants seven thousand and nine, and two hundred singing men and singing women.

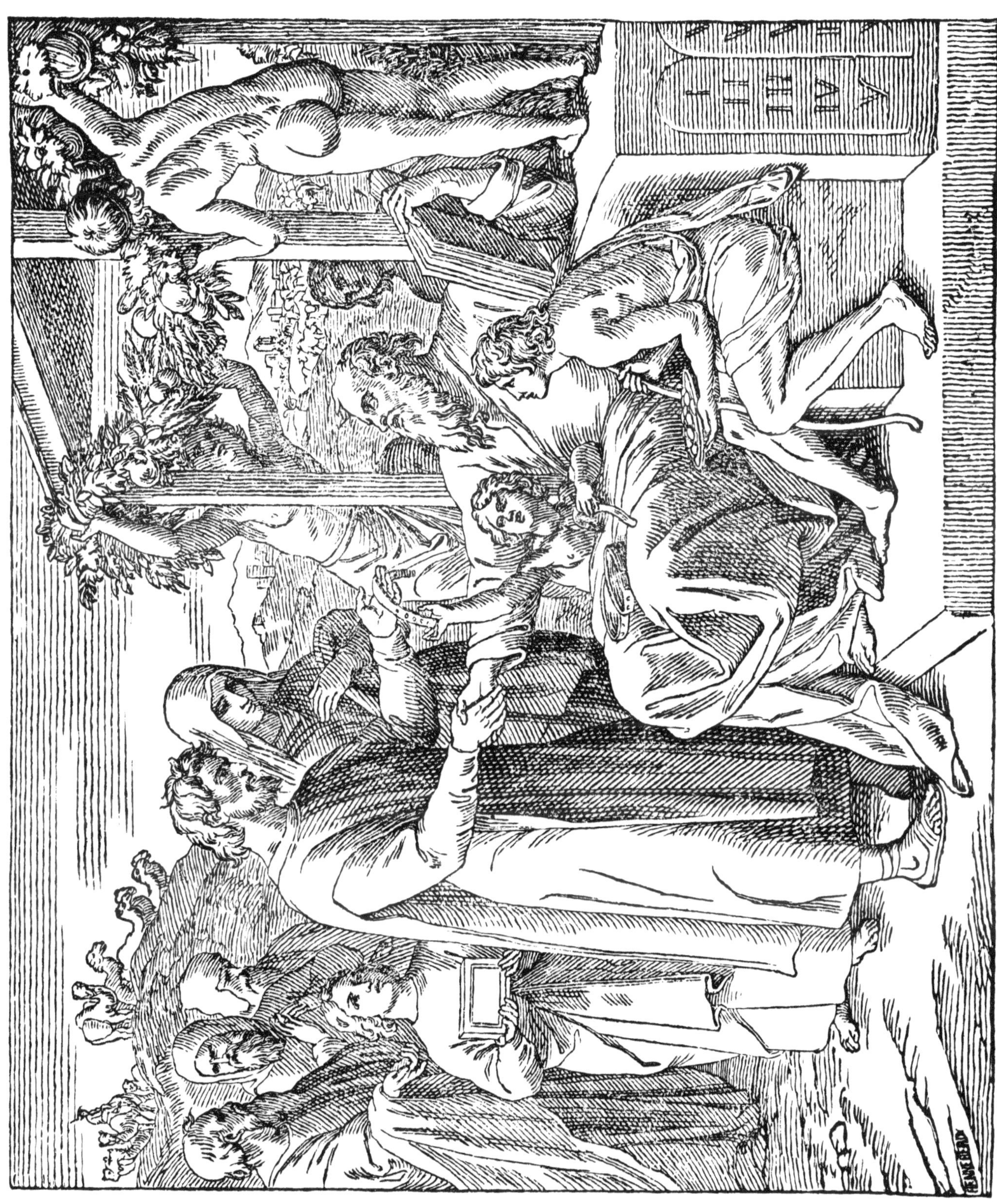

Job Visited by His Relatives

There came unto Job all his brethren, and all his sisters, and all they that had been of his acquaintance, and did eat bread with him in his house: and they comforted him. Every man also gave him a piece of money, and every one an earring of gold. And the Lord gave Job twice as much as he had before, so the Lord blessed the latter end of Job.

www.ingramcontent.com/pod-product-compliance
Lightning Source LLC
LaVergne TN
LVHW060619110826
845147LV00019B/1054

* 9 7 8 1 9 3 7 5 6 4 0 8 7 *